PRAISE FOR

Forgiving Our Parents, Forgiving Ourselves

This book is a must-read for all of us who are committed to helping people become whole.
Bill Hybels
Founding pastor, Willow Creek Community Church
South Barrington, Illinois

Without guidance, forgiving our parents and ourselves is easier said than done. Not an easy task no matter how old you are! In *Forgiving Our Parents, Forgiving Ourselves* my friend David Stoop has provided practical, doable steps for anyone who seeks forgiveness of others and self. David Stoop identifies what true forgiveness is and isn't—a key element in "getting over it and moving on." Truly a must-read for everyone, no matter how his or her upbringing may be defined.
Gary Smalley
Bestselling author, *Guarding Your Child's Heart*

With the help of this book, you can discover a new way of healing for yourself.
Archibald Hart
Psychologist and author, *Me, Myself and I*

This resource is refreshingly insightful with new perspectives on family and forgiveness. This practical book will impact any reader and is a welcome addition to Dave Stoop's other materials.
H. Norman Wright
Grief and trauma therapist
Bestselling author, *The Complete Guide to Trauma Counseling* and *Helping Those in Grief*

forgiving our parents forgiving ourselves

THE DEFINITIVE GUIDE
REVISED & UPDATED

DR. DAVID STOOP

Regal

From Gospel Light
Ventura, California, U.S.A.

Published by Regal
From Gospel Light
Ventura, California, U.S.A.
www.regalbooks.com
Printed in the U.S.A.

Library of Congress Cataloging-in-Publication Data
The Library of Congress has catalogued the first edition as follows:
Stoop, David A.
Forgiving our parents, forgiving ourselves : breaking generational patterns /
David Stoop
p. cm.
ISBN 978-0-8307-5723-7
1. Generational Patterns in Families—Psychology. 2. Problem families—
Psychological aspects. 3. Forgiveness.
RC455.4.F3S7852004
362.82'4-dc22
2003028052

Rights for publishing this book outside the U.S.A. or in non-English languages
are administered by Gospel Light Worldwide, an international not-for-profit ministry.
For additional information, please visit www.glww.org, email info@glww.org, or write to
Gospel Light Worldwide, 1957 Eastman Avenue, Ventura, CA 93003, U.S.A.

To order copies of this book and other Regal products in bulk quantities,
please contact us at 1-800-446-7735.

CONTENTS

INTRODUCTION

"If Dad were around today and did to us what he did back then, he'd be charged with child abuse."

"No way!" I countered. "Not our dad!"

"Think about it," my sister replied. Then she hung up.

That terse conversation took place more than 30 years ago, but I remember it as though it happened yesterday. The moment my sister slammed down the receiver was the moment my bubble burst. For years I had thought my dad was a good father. Now, I suddenly found I could do so no longer. He had been dead for 20 years at the time of our angry conversation. I did not particularly like to talk about him, for I had very little of him to hold onto in my memory. So I was not about to let anyone—not even my sister—destroy what little I had left.

Her remark about child abuse had to do with the way Dad used a belt when he spanked us—or at least when he spanked *me*. I never believed that he spanked *her* at all; according to my recollection, I took the blame for everything she did. I'm sure she remembered it differently. Dad believed in spanking. The only problem was that the spankings always came with a heavy overlay of anger and a lot of physical abuse.

Getting spanked by my father always followed a familiar pattern—almost a sort of ritual. Something would go wrong, and he'd look at me with that stern glare and snap, "Get down to the basement." I knew what *that* meant. There was no way to talk him out of it. Begging didn't work. I know, because I had tried it many times. Even offering an explanation was useless.

I can still remember how I felt, slouching down the basement stairs with him close behind me. First, he'd take off his belt; then he'd sit on a chair in the middle of the room. I'd bend over. Then I'd get the belt across my backside.

My dad would remain silent through all of this. If I cried too much, I'd get more. If I didn't cry *enough,* I'd get more. I remember working out a system for knowing how much crying was "enough." I'd wail away until he warned me to stop "before he gave me something to cry *about.*" That was my cue to quit, perhaps with a few final sniffles thrown in for good measure.

Once or twice I tried to stuff a book or magazine down my pants before heading downstairs. Despite the fact that our family went to church every Sunday, I wasn't exactly what you'd call a "praying man." But at those moments I'd pray earnestly that Dad wouldn't notice. One time he didn't notice until he was almost finished whipping me. He icily ordered me to take the book out. Then he spanked me for that infraction as well.

Up until that conversation with my sister, I never gave much thought to those spanking incidents. Actually, compared to what some of my friends reported about the way they got disciplined, I didn't think the treatment I got was all that unusual. *Everybody* got spanked by his or her parents in those days. And I don't suppose I really wanted to spend much time recalling the sick, scared feeling in my stomach when the time came to "go downstairs."

Still, when I was getting spanked, at least I had my dad's attention. For the most part, he always seemed too tired or distracted to notice me or care about anything that interested me. He worked long hours in a factory. When he came home at night, he was extremely tired. On the weekends he spent most of his time keeping the house up, working until he was exhausted.

The rest of his time—what little there was—was spent in "Porchville." We lived in Cleveland, Ohio, in a small house with a porch across the front and a swing at one end of the porch. I can remember Dad sitting on that swing, reading the newspaper or just staring out across the lawn. When he was finished with the paper, he would go out to the garage to work on something. We never talked about much of anything. Dad never took time to play catch with me or to notice how I threw a ball or fielded a grounder.

He was emotionally absent—except when the time came to "go downstairs."

The interesting thing is that for years if you had asked me whether I'd had a happy childhood, I would have said yes without giving it a second thought. Were we close as a family? "Of course," would have been my answer. My parents took good care of us. We never lacked for anything important, even when Dad's factory was on strike. We were a good family.

Or were we? My sister's words on the phone suddenly made me feel less confident that we really *were* all that close, or that everything had really been all that wonderful. I did not like these new thoughts. They felt dangerous.

Like all people who have idealized a parent, I had let my dad off the hook in a number of ways. I had carefully created a picture of my family as a happy place, one where anything unpleasant could be readily explained away. I focused on remembering the good parts.

For example, because we were all so emotionally distant, I enjoyed a great deal of freedom and independence. I had newspaper routes from an early age, so I always had money. In summer, when school was out, I could hop on my bike in the morning and not come home until dinnertime. One of my special pleasures was going to symphony concerts all by myself, even in grade school. I'd ride the streetcar there and back.

It wasn't until years later—when I realized that I never allowed *my* kids that kind of freedom—that I began to have second thoughts about my family of origin. I came to see that the reason why I didn't grant my kids that kind of latitude was not simply because "times are different now." It had to do with the fact that in my mind, all that freedom was linked to a sense of emotional abandonment. I just knew I wanted my family to be *different*.

I worked hard at earning Dad's approval. One summer, when I was still in grade school, his major project was repainting our wood frame house. I found it fascinating. I wanted to do what my dad was doing, so I pestered him to let me help. I could paint the bottom rows of siding, I said. He wasn't interested. "You don't know anything about painting," he said. "Go play with your friends. I've got work to do."

Several weeks later I was attending a Vacation Bible School at church. The craft project was to build a birdhouse. If we finished it in time, we would get to paint it. I felt so proud when the teacher commented on how well I had painted my birdhouse. "You're an excellent painter," she said. "You even know how to hold the brush."

I couldn't wait to show the finished project to my dad. When I told him what the teacher had said, he responded with a quick glance and a barely audible "Hmmm." Then he went back to reading his paper.

I can still remember the hot shame on my cheeks. Why did I have to have such an old father, one who was always too tired to care about what I did?

As I grew to adulthood, I searched for answers, for some way to understand why my father was the way he was. I wanted to find out what he was like, and where he had come from.

He had come to the United States from Northern Ireland, I knew that much. I had always been proud of the fact that my dad was Irish, and my mom *mostly* Irish. But when I asked him about it, he would brush me off with a gruff, "I don't want to talk about it." I dreamt of someday going to Ireland. I once asked him if he ever wanted to go back. "Never!" was his standard reply.

Dad grew up in Northern Ireland during the tumultuous era that Leon Uris wrote about in his novel *Trinity*. It was a cruel, terrifying period of history. The few things Dad did say about Ireland were beyond my comprehension. He would talk about "the troubles," and about truckloads of bodies being dumped into the river. Then he would become silent, and nothing could get him talking again. He acted as though he wanted to forget his roots.

But other things he did seemed to belie his disinterest in his heritage. Sometimes I would find him sitting in the living room, next to the radio, listening to the Queen of England speaking on a Canadian station. I remember thinking to myself, "Why is he so interested in what the Queen is saying if he won't even talk about where he grew up?"

I dug around, asked questions and pried loose whatever scraps of information I could. I learned that my father's father had died when Dad was only 13 (though I could never learn *how* he died). It became Dad's job to take care of his mother at that point. When the family came to America years later, it was still his job to look after her. It was through reading Uris's book that I learned of the old Irish tradition of the youngest son taking care of the widowed mother. Dad had no life of his own until he was 33. That was when his mother died. He met and married my mother when he was 35.

I worked hard at maintaining my idealized picture of my father. I started at an early age and kept at it long after he died. Now, even after talking with my sister, as I struggled with my hurt and anger toward this man who had passed away so many years before, I found I still wanted to let him off the hook. I could still explain away most of what I remembered.

My studies in developmental psychology only reinforced my rationalizations. It was clear to me that my dad had lived a painful childhood. He knew little of intimacy or closeness in his family. His mother, I learned, had been a large, domineering woman who had controlled his life for 33 years. His brothers and sisters had gone off and built lives of their own, but not him. How, then, could I expect him to know how to relate any better to me?

But after the conversation with my sister, it suddenly became more difficult to believe the things I told myself about Dad. I finally had to admit it; he had failed me and injured me in many ways. Yes, there were reasons. Yes, it may not have been "all his fault." But it still hurt!

I began having angry confrontations with him in my mind as I was driving, or lying awake in the middle of the night. I told him all the things I had wanted from him that he never gave me. I let him know how afraid I was of him, how I tried to stay out of his way in order to avoid his unpredictable temper. I told him how much I missed having a father who was interested in me and in what I was doing. I found myself, 20 years later, grieving over his death—something I had been unable to do at the time he died.

I wrote down some of the conversations that coursed through my mind, and related them to some people I trusted. As I did, the burden of pain and anger seemed to lift. I was surprised to discover that the image I held of my father did not disappear. If anything, he became more real, more complete. I still saw a father who had disappointed and injured me. But I also saw a man with strength and goodness in him. My new image, I felt certain, was much closer to reality.

But even though I had worked through my "father issues," the process still felt incomplete somehow. The bubble of idealization had burst. But I didn't feel settled. There was one more step needed to complete the process. I needed to *forgive* my father.

Why? Wasn't he dead and gone? What would be the point of forgiveness in such a situation? What was to be gained? The answers to these questions helped me come to a whole new understanding of what forgiveness is all about. Working through the issues raised by my own experience laid the foundation for much of the work I now do with patients in the clinic, for my workshops and seminars and for this book. *Forgiveness,* I have learned, *is the key to resolving the pain of the past and breaking generational patterns.* Without it, nothing is ever laid to rest. The past still operates in the present.

My own time of grappling with these issues came just as I was starting in practice as a psychologist. I was bothered by the fact that despite my best and most determined efforts to have things be "different" in my own family, I was noticing in myself the same kind of detachment toward my children that my father had shown toward me. I became intensely interested in how families worked and why patterns of relating that were hated and despised nevertheless got passed along from generation to generation. The study of family therapy provided a framework for solving these riddles, not only in my life but in the lives of the people I worked with.

The issues you face regarding your parents will be different than mine. They may be far more painful and damaging. But as you read this book, I want you to know that I have walked the path of hurt, confusion and pain that you now walk—and that I also know the release that will come as you follow the path of forgiveness. It was not until I worked through the process of forgiving my father, both for what he did and for what he did not do, that I felt our relationship was settled. And when that happened, I found that some other important relationship issues got settled for me as well, including a new openness to my own family.

A word of encouragement: Many people are put off by the word "forgiveness." Don't be. The purpose of this book is to explain what forgiveness is really all about. We'll see that its greatest value lies in what it does *within us,* and that forgiveness need not have anything at all to do with those who have hurt us until later—if, indeed, it needs to involve them at all. Forgiveness is for *us.* It sets us free.

PART ONE

Unpacking Family Baggage

1

Family: Ties that Bind?

The pain and heartache you may have suffered in your family may tempt you to put your family behind you once and for all. But "leaving home" is not that easy and may not be the healthiest course of action, anyway.

Brian was clearly in a bad way. By the time he came to see me, he had been hospitalized four separate times for the same set of problems: severe depression, alienation and thoughts of suicide. The hospital programs had all done their best, applying every conceivable form of individual treatment and therapy. Brian would get better and improve enough to be released from the hospital and sent home. But before long his symptoms would reappear and he would be right back where he started.

We talked for a long time. I asked him a lot of questions about himself, his feelings, his problems. I also asked him about his family. Much experience has taught me that family patterns can sometimes unlock mysteries that have yielded to no other attempts at understanding. One of the things he told me was that several years before—just prior to his first hospitalization—his cousin Sheila had tried to commit suicide. Her father was a police officer, and she had taken his gun and gone to an open field and shot herself.

The attempt had failed, and she was left permanently handicapped as a result. Brian spoke bitterly about the way his family blamed *him* for what had happened to his cousin. It seems that a week before she tried to kill herself, Sheila had talked to Brian about how hopeless she felt, how alone and depressed. Brian had been alarmed. He had asked her if she was contemplating suicide. She had insisted vehemently that she was not. Then, a week later, she made her futile but destructive attempt.

When the family heard about Brian's conversation with Sheila, they were outraged. Surely he should have seen what was coming! Surely he should have insisted that Sheila seek help! Surely he should have *told* someone what was going on! The fact that Sheila had specifically denied that she was thinking of suicide meant nothing. It was all his fault—or so the family seemed to think. And so, in time, did Brian. No one ever seemed to blame her father for leaving his gun carelessly available for her to take.

Brian was only 15 years old at the time and could not possibly have been expected to recognize his cousin's cry for help, but he felt responsible for what had happened. His parents, his aunts and uncles—they were right. It *was* his fault. He *was* to blame for Sheila's tragic condition. The feelings of remorse and guilt were almost enough to—quite literally—drive him crazy.

During the course of our time together, I was able to point out to Brian the pattern that seemed to have developed regarding his problems. When he went into the hospital where, of course, he was away from his family, he got better. But when he got out and went back home to live, it was only a matter of months until his family's attitudes toward him pushed him back into despair and depression.

I talked to Brian about *dysfunctional family systems—generational patterns*—of behaviors and relationships within families that work to make us unhealthy rather than healthy. I talked to him about the roles that members of such families take on, and the effects those roles can have on them. In particular, I talked to him about the role of scapegoat—the one onto whom all the others project their own feelings of guilt and shame. The more we talked, the clearer it became to Brian and to me that his problems stemmed, for the most part, from some very unhealthy behaviors and attitudes in his family. In time we were able to identify a number of these family patterns and dynamics. Brian had to change the way he responded to these patterns if he was to remain healthy. There were other factors, of course: the treatment and therapy provided in the hospital played an important role. But in Brian's case, family issues were the key. As we worked to resolve them, his other problems became more manageable and his life more stable.

> *Children don't know what causes their misery.*
> *In fact, children don't realize their dysfunctional home*
> *is abnormal. Even physically abused kids don't realize,*
> *while young, that normal parents don't beat their kids;*
> *they think that there is no other way to live.*
> NANCY CURTIS, *BEYOND SURVIVAL*[1]

Julie came from what most people would consider a perfectly "normal" family. On the outside, her parents looked like the classic "Ozzie and Harriet" couple. Her mother and father were still faithfully married to each other. Her father provided well for the family. Her mother never worked, preferring to stay home and care for the children. But on the inside, there were subtle dynamics at work in Julie's family that made it a difficult place to live.

One day, Julie poured out her pain over one especially vivid memory. She was about four years old, and she was walking somewhere with her parents. They were arguing about something—Julie never knew about what—and all at once her mother simply started walking away. Julie's father suddenly turned and yelled at *Julie*. He grabbed her by the shoulders, shook her and threw her down on the sidewalk. Then he stomped away.

Julie's mother froze in her tracks. For what seemed like forever, she simply stood there, staring at Julie, then at Julie's father. Finally she motioned for Julie to come to her. Julie ran to her mother in tears and clung to her, sobbing.

A few minutes later, Julie and her mother came around a corner and found her father standing there, about 20 feet away, his hands in his pockets, his head down, shuffling his feet awkwardly. "He looked like a hurt little boy," Julie said, "like a little boy who knew he had done a bad thing and didn't know what to do about it."

Neither Julie's mother nor her father said a word. They just *silently* fell in and started walking again. Julie remembers her father reaching out to tousle her hair. She drew back, still trembling with fear from his recent outburst. But her mother seemed to have forgotten all about it. The three of them walked along together, her mother holding hands with Julie's father on one side and with Julie on the other. Years later, Julie could still remember the confusion she felt, the empty, hurt feeling inside. How could her father treat her like that? How could her mother *let* him? And how could both of them simply go on *as if nothing had happened?*

As I listened to Julie talk, I wondered to myself how many other times that scene had been played out. How many times was she angrily shoved aside, bearing the brunt of a parent's pent-up anger? How many times, I wondered, had her *father* been similarly shoved aside, his fears and hurts ignored, when *he was* a child? Julie had described him as looking like "a hurt little boy." I suspected there was more truth to that characterization than she knew.

And what about Julie's mother? What did her behavior say about the way she had learned to deal with conflict? Evidently she had learned not to confront, but to simply stand back, stay silent and wait for the storm to pass. Julie described her as literally caught between the two people who were the most important to her, silently enduring their crises, hoping for the best.

In time Julie and I were able to learn more about both her own family and about her parents' families. We could see how patterns of behavior had been passed *cross-generationally* to both parents, and then on to her. She came to understand how her mother's *peacemaker* role prevented clean, clear resolution of problems. She came to recognize how *unspoken rules* in her family prevented everyone from talking about what they were experiencing, and from dealing with unpleasant realities. As Julie worked through the pain of her new awareness, she gradually discovered a wonderful freedom from unhealthy self-concepts and destructive emotions that had plagued her all her life.

Mary's story was more traumatic. Her depression was so severe and so long-standing that it was hard for her to dig through the layers of emotional calluses she had built up and come to grips with her family background.

That background was a nightmare. Her father was an alcoholic. Her mother was physically abusive; Mary told how she had once beaten her with a metal towel rack. Both parents were verbally abusive. Mary told of the relief she felt when they would go out and leave her and her older brother home alone. But even that soon led to other problems.

When Mary was eight years old, her brother raped her. Later, when her mother came home, Mary sobbed as she told her what had happened. Her mother never even checked Mary's physical condition. When the brother denied having done anything wrong, Mary's mother called *her* a liar and sent her to her room. Both Mary and her brother learned the *lesson* of this incident: that the sexual abuse could continue and that Mary would endure in silence. Once this issue came to light, however, it was easy for Mary to see how the *law of silence* had held her prisoner all her life.

Lydia, by contrast, came to counseling knowing full well that she needed to deal with issues of sexual abuse. Her stepfather had molested her from the time she was 12 until she left home at age 16. Her mother knew what was happening but did nothing about it. She simply waited in another room until it was over. Sometimes she even watched it occur.

After spending several months working through this issue, Lydia's therapist arranged for her mother and stepfather to come to a combined session with their daughter. Lydia had written down what she wanted to say to them. She had practiced with her counselor how she would say it. There would be no hysterical name-calling or exaggerated accusation, just a straightforward recitation of what had happened and how it had made her feel. Lydia and her therapist felt that taking this step was important if Lydia was to let go of her bitterness and get free of her past.

Lydia's parents sat silently through her presentation. When she finished, they stoically denied everything—both of them! They were quite calm and matter-of-fact about it. The only emotion they showed was irritation that Lydia had accused them of "such terrible things" in front of a stranger. In some ways, Lydia had run into a brick wall. She went back to the group and talked through her disappointment at her parents' denial. As she worked through her feelings, she was also able to see why she had been held hostage by her past for so long.

Larry spent most of the first five years of his life waiting. Usually, he was sitting in the backseat of a car, waiting for his parents to emerge, thoroughly drunk, from some bar. He became accustomed to being left behind. One day he stood on his aunt's front porch and watched his parents drive away and leave him yet again. But this time was different: this time they never came back.

As bad as those first five years had been, they were overshadowed by the questions that haunted him into adulthood. Where did his parents go? Why did they leave him? Where were they now? No one in Larry's family knows the answer to those questions. Larry has had to learn how to deal with the gaping hole left by his parents' *abandonment* of him. When he came to counseling he was burned out from trying so hard to win everyone's approval. Slowly he started to see that his present lifestyle was directly connected to his fear of being abandoned and the experiences of his childhood.

Generational Patterns

The people we have just described, and many others whose stories we could recount, are unique individuals with distinctly different backgrounds and life circumstances. No two are alike in every respect. But they are all alike in one very important respect: They are all products of families whose dynamics and relational patterns were sufficiently disordered that they can be considered unhealthy and dysfunctional.

They are grown men and women who, after years of struggling with a variety of emotional, psychological and relational problems, have come to realize that part of the reason they "are the way they are" is because something in their family background made them that way. Usually there are additional factors involved as well. But in all these cases, and in many others besides, family dynamics wound up holding the key to recovery. As these men and women have come to understand more clearly the way these dynamics have affected them, they have been able to cut themselves loose from their effect and go on to live happier, more fruitful lives.

The stories I have cited are drawn from my experience as a professional counselor. Some are obviously more dramatic and traumatic than others. But some—like the story of Julie, the little girl whose father shoved her in a fit of anger—do not seem dramatic at all. There the family dysfunction was less extreme, less outwardly visible. *But it was no less real.* I am convinced that a great many of us, once we know what to look for and how to interpret it, can gain from understanding the dysfunctional dynamics of our own family—whether or not our past has been scarred by such obvious forms of dysfunction as physical and sexual abuse, divorce and the like.

However, to say that families are dysfunctional is redundant. Every family is dysfunctional to some degree because everything that human beings touch is to some degree dysfunctional. "Dysfunctional" means that something doesn't work the way it was intended. Each of us, because of Adam's sin, doesn't work quite the way God designed us to work. Our families, our work, even our play is less than perfect because of sin.

The problem, of course, is that we live in an imperfect world. We were *all* raised by imperfect parents in imperfect families. And, if we are honest, we recognize that we have all grown up to be imperfect adults. There is thus a sense in which we can *all* justifiably see ourselves as "adult children of dysfunctional families."

I often say that I grew up in a dysfunctional family and that when I married and had children, I created a new dysfunctional family. Now I watch my sons create their own dysfunctional families. Our goal is not to stop being dysfunctional—that we cannot do. Our goal is to become more and more healthy in the ways we function as a family. I have worked hard to make my family healthier than the family I grew up in, and I trust my sons are working to make their families healthier than what they experienced growing up.

Therefore, it is probably more helpful to say that some families are healthier in the way they operate than other families. And some are unhealthier than others. So if you are having a problem with whether or not your family was dysfunctional, assume that it was and is. Then look to see how healthy or how unhealthy your family was and probably still is.

You may feel that your family of origin wasn't dysfunctional since your father wasn't an alcoholic. . . . The truth is, however, that, due to the fallen nature of all parents (and children), all families are flawed and therefore dysfunctional to a certain degree. Addictive and compulsive behaviors (addictions to food, sex, work, and so on) are extremely common in even "the best of families," and such behavior is almost always linked to some form of dysfunctional family background.

DAVE CARDER, ET AL., *SECRETS OF YOUR FAMILY TREE*[2]

A definition that includes everything and excludes nothing is not a very helpful definition. Let's recognize, then, that I am describing a condition with a range of expressions. You may consider yourself a product of what one man calls "your basic, everyday, garden-variety dysfunctional family." You recognize that your parents had their flaws and your family its weaknesses, but you have never felt that they have negatively affected your adult life in a major way. Most people who place themselves in this category are surprised when they discover how big were the "little" hurts they endured and how they affected their life. If you place yourself in this category, I encourage you to read this book for the insights you can gain into how to make your own life even more fruitful, and how to make your family life even more satisfying.

Others have already recognized that this is a book about *them.* As you read the stories of Brian, Mary, Lydia and the others, you heard bells go off inside your head, and something inside you said,

That's me *he's talking about. That's* my *life he's describing.* If you are in this category, I believe this book can help you begin a wonderful process of growth and recovery.

Still others will be unsure at this point. You may never have heard the phrase "dysfunctional family" before, let alone understand what it means or how it may apply to you. All you know is that something is not right in your life. It may be anything from a lingering depression, to a problem with anger, to bouts of extreme anxiety, to inexplicable difficulties trusting others and getting close to them in relationships. You may have tried a number of things to deal with your problem, with varying degrees of success. You may be a deeply religious person whose commitment to spiritual truth has provided a great deal of comfort, but still you find yourself groping for the key to some personal difficulties that continues to elude you. If you place yourself in this category, I urge you to read this book carefully. It may well mark the beginning of an exciting time of self-discovery and growth for you.

Family: Who Needs It?

Let's get back to the men and women whose stories opened this chapter. Given the amount of pain and anguish their parents caused them, why don't they just "put it all behind them"? That's really the big question. Many of us, when we look at the problems we continue to experience because of our imperfect backgrounds, are tempted to feel this way. Aren't we grown-ups now? Aren't we able to think and act and decide for ourselves? Why not just leave our family of origin behind? Why not just forget about it and get on with life? We don't want to open up problem areas, so why think about them?

I often work with people who have moved from the east coast to the west coast just to get away from their parents and their family. What they don't realize is that when they moved, part of the baggage they brought with them was their family. Their parents are like a committee that lives inside their head. Moving away geographically doesn't change anything—the committee is still active. Distance doesn't really change anything.

We *can't* just walk away and pretend that our family never happened. (Indeed, as we go on, we will see that *trying* to "walk away and pretend it never happened" is one of the *worst* things we can do.) Every person I have met from an unhealthy family system goes through a period when they are so grieved and angry about what has happened to them that they feel they never want anything to do with their parents again. Yet they constantly find themselves drawn back. Deep inside, they find they still want something, still *need* something from their families. The question is, why? Why does our family still exert such a strong grip on us even as adults?

To answer that question, we need to look back on our original experience of family. In the beginning of our life, family is indispensable for two reasons: first, for our sheer survival; second, for our early development and socialization.

It takes only a brief glance at an infant to recognize the survival aspect. Unlike most species in the animal kingdom, which shove their offspring out of the nest within a matter of weeks or months, human beings are so created that they are dependent on their parents (or some other adult member of the species) for their survival for many years.

But even as we grow older, our "family ties" continue. Because we are so needy at such a young age, we develop extraordinarily tight bonds to our family, even in those cases when it was harmful to us. Our neediness continues when we become adults, even though it usually takes different forms. This is a constant reminder of our original dependence on our family.

As hard as we may try to deny our neediness as adults, it is still there, exerting its tug on our psyche, always drawing us back to our original tie to the family. Consider the familiar case of the young adult who cannot wait to get away from his parents but who, once he has done so, is forever coming back for home-cooked meals, for money and (though he would never admit it) for parenting.

The longing for family is incredibly powerful, even in those cases where it might seem least warranted. Lydia, for example, knew full well what her mother and stepfather were like. She knew the pain she had experienced at their hands. Deep down, I think she knew how unlikely it was that they would ever acknowledge the damage done to her, let alone take any responsibility for it. Yet she longed for their love and affection. The longing never went away, even after the disastrous session in which they blandly denied the shocking behavior she knew to be true.

> *Many of us left home, defiantly vowing, "I'll never do it like my parents." Unfortunately, we are what we learn, and eventually, somehow, our parents manage to take up residence inside us. Only later as adults do we discover that we have never truly left home. In fact, in many ways we are just like our parents, who played the same game, different name—yet all products of a codependent heritage, "Lost in the shuffle."*
> ROBERT SUBBY, *LOST IN THE SHUFFLE*[3]

If these longings for family exist in us as children toward our parents, surely they must also exist in parents toward their children. The overwhelmingly powerful instinct of mother love is familiar to all of us. I have never met a parent who, at some level, did not want to love his offspring. I have met some who did not *know how* to do it, many who simply *failed* to do it and many who had lost heart and felt they no longer wanted to make the effort. But I have never met one who would not acknowledge a deep—sometimes almost desperate—desire to be "a good mom or dad."

If parents feel this way, if they long for closeness with their children this much, then why do they do so many destructive things to them? Part of the answer may lie in the parents' own early experience in their families—of the generational patterns they experienced.

Ray, for example, told me of the rage and hatred he felt toward his father during his late teenage years. Once, when he was 18, he invited his father to go for a walk with him. He was planning, quite literally, to kill his father. His parents lived out in the woods of the Pacific Northwest. Ray tucked a gun in his belt in the small of his back. As they walked together, and as he contemplated what he was about to do, he decided to ask his father for the first time why he had been so brutally abusive toward him.

"Tears welled up in his eyes when I asked him that," Ray remembered. "I was shocked. I'd never picked up the slightest trace of softness or sentiment in him before. He told me that his father—my grandfather—had done the very same things to him when he was a boy. His father would beat him with a horsewhip. Grandpa even whipped Grandma once, when she tried to stop him from hurting my dad."

Ray and his father walked along in silence for a few moments. Then his father turned to him and said, "You know, Ray, there were times when I just wanted to kill him."

Ray's murderous rage subsided after that. But his confusion grew. He felt sorrow for what his father had been through, even as he continued to feel anger toward him. Most of all, he grappled with understanding his father's behavior. "Why would he do the very same things to me that his father did to him?" Ray asked. (A good question, and one that we will try to answer as we go along.)

The Fractured Family

It is not news that the family structure has changed. Instead of the proverbial large extended family living together on the family farm—or at least close by—most families now live in urban or suburban settings with only the immediate family close by. An increasing number of these are single-parent families. In almost all cases, the support and care once provided by the extended family now come from friends and acquaintances—if it is to be found at all.

As the family has been changing, it also has increasingly become the object of study and concern. Scholars have generated vast piles of statistics to describe *what* has happened. But their figures, charts and graphs offer us little help in understanding *why* it has happened or what we can do about it. We know in excruciating detail how the divorce rate has skyrocketed, only recently showing signs of slowing down. We know how many more children are suffering the trauma of family collapse. But we don't know very much about how to change the trends or about how to help the survivors recover.

Added to these changes is the changing place of women in our culture. Women have won some equality concerning their economic and social standing. But the effects of these changes have yet to be integrated into the family. Researchers still vigorously debate how—or even whether—the New Woman can be part of the Traditional Family.

Whether all these changes are good or bad is beside the point of our present consideration. The fact is that the changes *are* happening at such a dizzying pace that the family has not been able to keep up with them.

That the family is in trouble requires no proof. We have only to listen to friends and co-workers, or even to examine our own concerns and struggles, to know that the family as we have known and understood it is under attack. Young people increasingly are afraid to get married; they do not want to risk repeating the patterns of disillusionment and despair they have seen in their parents' generation. Or, if they do marry, many decide not to have children for the same reasons.

Clearly, something is wrong. But how do we define what is right?

The Normal Family

What is a "normal" family? Is it the two-parent, 2.3-child unit that came to seem so common in the "Baby Boom" years of the late 1940s and 1950s? Or the extended clan immortalized by such television programs as *The Waltons*?

It is more difficult to answer these questions than it might seem at first. The birth of the family predates recorded history. Even in Genesis, the first book in the Bible, the family is more *assumed* than *explained*. Indeed, Genesis offers examples of many different types of families throughout its pages. Anthropology offers a similarly varied picture. There seem to be as many different patterns of "the family" as there are different human cultures.

Nevertheless, there *are* some elements that all these family types have in common. By focusing on them, we can at least arrive at an understanding of "family" that can serve as a basis for our discussion in this book.

One common element is the bonding of a particular man and woman in a relationship that is understood, at some level, to be stable and exclusive. In most cultures with which we are familiar—especially in those built on the foundation of a Christian world-view—this takes the form of marriage.

The other common element is the parent-child relationship. There is an understanding that the offspring produced by the union of a particular man and woman "belong" to them in some unique sense and are their specific responsibility to care for and raise.

There are, of course, variations on these patterns. In our own day we are quite familiar with the single-parent family. But even this pattern, common as it is, is almost universally regarded as a departure from the ideal. Almost no one proposes that single-parent families ought to be the norm for everyone. Other variations—communal families, for example, with a large group of adults accepting equal responsibility for a large group of children—have also been attempted, usually with little success. Again, few would propose them as a universal norm.

Thus, we seem to arrive at a very basic concept of what constitutes a "normal" family. Indeed, the almost instinctive tendency of human beings to gravitate toward a two-parent plus children model of the family—augmented in various ways by the presence of extended family members ranging from grandparents to uncles, aunts and cousins—suggests that such an arrangement has been "designed into" the human race by a wise and loving God. Since our aim is to examine the effects that family dynamics have on children, especially when those children have themselves grown to adulthood, we will focus on the parent-child component of the "normal" family. By understanding the basic goals of parenting, we can refine our understanding of what the "normal" family looks like.

Our first task in life—the first job we set out to do, beginning at the moment we enter this world from the womb—is to form a secure attachment with a figure who will make the world a safe and reliable place for us. Ordinarily, of course, this is the mother, since the newborn has spent nine months in a symbiotic connection to her. But the father also plays a crucial role in this. Both parents are to be attachment figures for the infant. So we can say that one norm for a healthy family is that it provides a loving environment in which the child can learn to trust.

When we are about six or eight months old, we begin to work on our second task in life, which is to define ourselves as separate, unique individuals within this context of love and trust. This is sometimes referred to as "individuation," the process of discovering what it is that "makes me, *me.*" Our ability to accomplish this second task will be directly related to how much love and security we have experienced in the earlier process of bonding with our parents and our environment. (We'll look at this process more closely in chapter 3.)

Since unconditional love is the basis for all that occurs at later stages, we can round out our definition of the normal family by saying that it is a place where we can experience an unconditional love that gives us both the security and the freedom to successfully become autonomous individuals.

The Family Covenant

An example of this kind of relationship can be found in the ancient concept of *covenant.* A covenant was a type of relationship in which the parties each committed themselves, totally and unilaterally, to faithfulness.

The word "unilaterally" is important. In most relationships and agreements, each party feels bound to the relationship only so long as the other party "holds up his end of the deal." If the other person fails to live up to his or her part of the bargain, then I (the first party) am excused from living up to my part. (In our society, this is the way contracts work.) Not so in a covenant. In a covenant relationship, each party has certain duties and obligations that he or she is obligated to fulfill *even if the other party fails to come through.*

The place from which most of the Western world today draws its understanding of covenant is the Bible, which speaks of two kinds of covenants. The first is a covenant between two (or more) people who are on an equal footing with one another. A business agreement, for example, could be in the form of a covenant. The most obvious instance of this kind of covenant, of course, is marriage.

A second kind of covenant involved an unconditional offer from a lord to a vassal, in which the lord promised to protect and care for the vassal. A king might make such a covenant with his subjects. Another example of this kind of covenant relationship was between God and the Jews. It is easy to see how this kind of covenant exemplifies what is supposed to happen between parents and children.

Thus we can say that the family is meant to be an intersection of two covenants: a "horizontal" covenant between husband and wife, and a "vertical" covenant between parents and children. Again, we will be focusing on the parent-child dimension in this book. But both dimensions are important, for without them it is impossible to create the environment of unconditional love—some would call it a community—in which human beings can grow as autonomous individuals.

It is important to note that the existence of a covenant does not mean that a relationship will be free of discord. Quite the opposite. As in any human relationship, the parties to a covenant will have their ups and downs, their trials and struggles. The difference is that they are committed to working through these difficulties and trying to resolve them. The bonds of covenant are often tested. They can be broken. But they can also be restored. It is also important to understand that the bonds of covenant love, and the effects of their being broken, can extend across generations. Each individual family, each parent-child bond, is but one link in a chain that extends both backward and forward in time. As we examine the *effects* of growing up in a dysfunctional family, we will need to trace the ways in which our parents may have been similarly impacted by *their* families. And we will want to understand how we, in turn, can avoid passing on a legacy of family dysfunction to our own children.

When we talk about dysfunctional families then, this is what we mean: situations in which the bonds of covenant love, especially between parents and children, have been strained or broken. How those breakdowns occurred and how the bonds can be restored (and the ill effects of the breakdown reversed) are the main topics of this book.

Freedom and Change

Let's summarize what we have said so far. All of us are deeply influenced by our families. All of our families are imperfect—perhaps more so today than ever, as the institution of the family has gone through unprecedented change and upheaval in recent decades. Some of us have come from families where the "imperfections" were significant enough to cause us noticeable difficulty in our adult lives. We are "adult children of dysfunctional families."

As much as we may try to cut ourselves free from our "family ties," their attachment runs too deep. Freedom lies in facing our problems squarely, in understanding as concretely as possible how our family fell short of the norm—how it failed to provide us with a community of unconditional love in which we could grow up healthy and strong. The goal of this is not to reinforce our self-pity or prompt us to hold our parents in contempt. As we shall see, clearer understanding enables us to take steps that will release us from the bondage of our past by enabling us to forgive those who have hurt us.

> *A necessary part of recovery is for us to gain a balanced perspective of those who raised us. We need to lift the veils of denial from our eyes and see the past as it was, not as we wish it might have been.*
> ROBERT SUBBY, *LOST IN THE SHUFFLE*[4]

The kind of family you came from can have a profound effect on a number of important dynamics in your personal life—even as an adult. We have all sometimes talked of "growing up and leaving home." But in many respects, "leaving home" is hard to do. Our families continue to exert influence on us long after we think we have left them behind. To the degree that our family was healthy, it is good news. To the degree that our family was dysfunctional, it can be bad news. Even so, freedom and change *are* possible. The key lies in understanding more thoroughly the dynamics of family life and how those dynamics have affected us. The next step in gaining this understanding is to learn to look at the family in a new way: as a *system*.

In the next chapter, you will read about Traci, a teenage runaway, whose problem became the key to unlocking the dynamics of a dysfunctional family system. Only when Traci and her parents understood the role she had been playing in the family as a system would they identify the root problem. And only then were real freedom and change possible.

KEY POINTS TO REMEMBER

1. Understanding your family background is the key to understanding yourself.

2. All families are dysfunctional in some way. It's better to talk about healthy and unhealthy families.

3. People move away from home to get away from their family; but in reality, they take their family with them.

4. Today, families are changing, as are the roles of men and women, but family is still an intersection of two covenants.

5. Your first task in life is to feel safe; i.e., experience attachment. The second task is to be separate; i.e., experience autonomy.

6. Personal freedom comes when you face your problems head-on.

Notes

1. Nancy Curtis, *Beyond Survival* (Lake Mary, FL: Strang Communications, 1990), pp. 27-28.
2. Dave Carder, et al., *Secrets of Your Family Tree* (Chicago: Moody Press, 1991), p. 15.
3. Robert Subby, *Lost in the Shuffle* (Deerfield Beach, FL: Health Communications, Inc., 1987), p. 92.
4. Ibid., p. 89.

The Family System

*A family is more than a group of individuals
who happen to share the same address and the same
last name. Many of the riddles of "why you are the
way you are" can be unlocked by looking at the
family as a system of relationships and
interpersonal dynamics.*

Traci's distraught parents had come for counseling because their 16-year-old daughter had run away from home many times, and had been gone for several weeks each time. Their worry was justifiable.

One traditional way of looking at the situation would have been to say that Traci herself had a problem and needed help. That was certainly the way her parents saw it. What was wrong with their daughter? Why did she take it into her head to act like this? What could be done to change her behavior? Their focus—again, understandably—was on her problems as an individual.

But their counselor was looking at the situation through different eyes. He saw Traci not just as an individual but also as part of a family, as one part of a larger picture. Whatever personal difficulties Traci might have—and there was no reason to doubt that she had them—it was likely that her behavior was also influenced by some dynamic in her family experience.

From hours of conversation with Traci, her two younger sisters and her parents, a pattern began to emerge. The parents' marriage was on thin ice. They fought a lot and had talked more than once about divorce. About two years before coming to the counselor, they had separated for a few months; and it was just after her father came back from that first separation that Traci ran away for the first time. The parents, while obviously aware of the difficulties they were experiencing in their own relationship, saw no correlation between that and Traci's troubling behavior. It was during a joint counseling session, with both Traci and her parents present, that the lid came off.

It began innocently enough. The counselor complimented Traci: "It's out of *loyalty* to your family that you keep running away, isn't it?" he said. "You're so concerned for their welfare that you're even willing to sacrifice your own safety." Traci blushed a bit and smiled, nodding her head ever so slightly. She seemed to understand what the counselor was saying.

Her parents, however, did not. They erupted in anger. "Loyalty?" they cried. "What has that got to do with anything? Why are you applauding her for running away from home?"

The counselor waited for the explosion to subside. "Well," he said, "during our discussions together, it has seemed clear to me that the only thing you two agree on is that Traci is a problem. In fact, it seems as though working on her problem is practically the only thing that holds you together.

"What I think is happening is this: Traci has somehow picked up that when she's doing okay, the two of you begin to experience and express your own problems more vigorously. I think she's concluded that the only way to hold the family together is for her to create a crisis that will force you to stick together. The fact is that your marriage problem has cast her in the role of 'family scapegoat.' When she runs away and causes you grief, she's just acting out the role she's been conditioned to play."

From that point, the theme of the counseling sessions shifted from *Traci* having a problem to the *family* having a problem, and then to the parents having the real problem. The parents came back for several sessions without the kids. They began the arduous process of addressing their own relationship and the way it impacted their children. At this point, they have made good progress, though they still have a long way to go. But they have learned an important lesson: They have learned how helpful it can be to view their family as a *system*.

The Family Organism

It was in the 1950s that some interesting psychiatrists and psychologists made a remarkable discovery about families. That was not what they set out to do, which was to study the behavior of patients who had been diagnosed as being schizophrenic. Among the things they did was to observe the patients interacting with their families.

What they saw astonished them. In many cases, what they had thought was a mental illness was not an illness at all. Much of the patients' behavior, when looked at by itself, seemed clearly disordered. But it could actually be seen as perfectly reasonable and orderly *in the context of the family*. In other words, it was the *family*, not just the individual, that was dysfunctional. To some degree, these apparently sick individuals acted the way they did because their role in the family prompted them to do so—much as Traci's role prompted her to become a chronic runaway. Thus arose the notion of seeing and assessing the family as a system.

A family is not merely a collection of separate individuals who simply happen to share the same last name and street address. The family is an organism in which the attitudes, values and actions of each member interact with those of all the other members. Each family member shapes, and is shaped by, the other family members. Each one is the way he or she is, in part, because of the way he or she fits into the overall scheme of things, the system. Many of our behavior patterns—both the healthy ones and the unhealthy ones—flow from the role we occupy in our particular family system. Understanding the family system, and the role we play in it, can unlock emotions and behaviors that would otherwise seem impossible to explain.

Tennessee Williams's classic play, *The Glass Menagerie*, offers a typical example of how a family system operates. Laura, the daughter in the play, could easily be considered mentally ill, even schizophrenic. But if we look at the world through her eyes—especially the world of her family—her "crazy" behavior becomes perfectly logical. Indeed, just as in Traci's case, her behavior is vital to the family's survival. Whenever the tension between her mother and brother rises to a dangerous level, Laura steps in with some bizarre type of behavior that takes the focus off their fighting and shifts it to her and her "strangeness."

Once we understand the concept of the family system, it is not so easy to say simply that Laura or Traci are "sick." Each may well have problems of her own that need to be addressed. However, a good case can be made that there is more to it than that, that each is the way she is because of the family she is part of. Again, it is the family that is sick, not just the individual members.

Linear and Interactive Thinking

You may remember learning in high school science class the principle that "for every action there is an equal and opposite reaction." This principle is an example of *linear* thinking: If I do "A," then "B" will happen. If it does not, then I know I have not done "A" correctly. This way of thinking is one of the basic foundations of modern science, and it is a tremendous help when you are trying to figure out what is going on in a laboratory.

Everything occurring in a family, regardless of how carefully it may be hidden, impacts the children. Everything.

ROBERT HEMFELT AND PAUL WARREN,
KIDS WHO CARRY OUR PAIN[1]

But it is less helpful when you are trying to figure out what is going on in a relationship, let alone in a family. In situations involving human beings, and especially human systems like a family, we have to learn to apply *interactive* thinking. We have to be aware that a given action on our part may or may not cause a given reaction on someone else's part. It may cause a reaction completely different from what we intended or expected. Or it may cause no reaction at all.

The reason is simple: We are dealing with other people, who have their own ideas, feelings and free will, all of which enter into the equation. Moreover, we are never dealing with them in a vacuum. An encounter between you and me isn't necessarily just between you and me. There will frequently be other people, other factors, affecting the situation.

One writer has said that the difference between linear thinking and interactive thinking is like the difference between kicking a tin can and kicking a dog.[2] When you kick a tin can, the results are fairly predictable. You can measure the force being transferred from your foot to the can, factor in the weight of the can and the wind conditions and calculate pretty accurately where the can will end up.

But kicking a dog is a different matter, simply because the dog has the capacity to act and react on its own. When you kick the dog, he may jump. He may politely get up and move over. He may get angry and snarl at you. Or (if he is like my dog), he may simply raise an eyebrow and look up at you as if to say, "Now why did you have to go and do that to poor, little me?"

Now imagine that there are two cats napping alongside the dog, a parrot in a cage in the next room and a group of children playing nearby, all who see the incident take place. When you kick the dog, any or all of these witnesses may react in any number of ways, none of which are fully predictable. You may think, when you kick the dog, that you know what will happen next. And you may turn out to be right. But it is more likely that the results will be different than you expected, unless you become very adept at understanding the "system" you are part of. The better you understand the system, the better you will be able to make predictions about it and adjust your actions in order to produce the results you seek.

All of this is precisely what we try to do when we look at a family as a system. Relationships among family members never proceed according to linear thinking. They are always interactive, and always occur in the context of a system. To use another old saying, "The whole is greater than the sum of its parts." There is more to how a family operates than just the personalities and tendencies of the individual members. Something special is created by the interrelatedness of family members, something that enters into every facet of family life.

Here is a simple illustration of how this works. Donna had a long-standing frustration with her husband, Fred. She was very social and outgoing. He was a quiet, withdrawn man who had few relational skills and little desire to develop any. They had been married for 15 years, and Donna had spent most of that time trying to get Fred to be more sociable.

She had tried everything. She got him to attend a Sunday School class at the church that had a lot of social events. She dragged him along month after month for years, until she finally got tired of the hassle and simply quit going to the class herself. She planned events with members of his family, thinking that would draw him out. She put all her plans and desires on hold, trying to figure out how to get Fred to change.

Nothing worked. In fact, it seemed that the harder she tried to get Fred to be more sociable, the more resolute he became about staying in his shell. He did not want to go out. He did not care about seeing his family or about doing things with other couples. Just let him go fishing once a year and he was content the rest of the time to simply go back and forth to work and enjoy a quiet life at home.

Donna was trapped in linear thinking. She figured that the way to move Fred in a certain direction was to give him a shove in that direction. If he did not move, then she simply needed to shove harder. What she did not realize was that *Fred was shoving back*. Every time she pushed him, he resisted. And the harder she pushed, the more stubbornly he resisted.

We pointed out to Donna that her experience reflected a basic reality of linear thinking—*that trying harder only gets you more of the same result*. We began to look at her relationship with Fred, not just in isolation but also as part of a broader family system. She began to grasp that action "A" does not necessarily produce result "B"; that there might be a host of other factors to take into consideration.

She began to realize that Fred's reclusive behavior pattern had been in place long before she met him. He grew up in a chaotic family, with an alcoholic father and a nagging mother. The way he had learned to cope with the chaos was to withdraw inside himself and stay out of things as much as possible. Even now, at his job, the relational dynamics were such that his best course of action often was to "lie low" to keep the boss off his back. In short, almost everything in Fred's life had taught him to deal with people—especially with people who were demanding something from him—by pretending he wasn't there.

By this point, Donna could see that her efforts to "help" Fred become more sociable only provoked this well-practiced response, and that trying harder to help him was only going to generate more of the same. This realization came as a tremendous relief. If she wasn't the cause of Fred's problem, and if she couldn't "fix" him by working on him, then she felt released to explore some of her own interests.

Interestingly enough, the minute Donna stopped working on Fred and began pursuing things she simply liked to do, Fred began to respond. Her nagging kept his reclusiveness in place. Now that she had given up the role of Family Nag, he seemed free to give up the role of Family Hermit. When he saw her doing things she wanted to do, without putting any pressure on him to join in, he started—very tentatively—to come out of hiding.

The Importance of Punctuation

Anyone who has ever taken a course in grammar knows how important punctuation is. The very same set of words can have entirely different meanings if the punctuation is changed. For example, take the following passage from the Bible: "Let him that stole steal no more . . . let him labour" (Eph. 4:28, *KJV*). Seems clear enough, doesn't it? But look what happens if we change the punctuation:

"Let him that stole, steal. No more let him labour." That's a very different message, isn't it? Yet it uses precisely the same words in precisely the same order. The only difference is the punctuation.

By the same token, our understanding of an event (or series of events) depends on the way we mentally "punctuate" it. Let's go back to Donna and Fred. Donna complained that she was unable to do what she wanted because Fred was so controlling by his passive behavior. Fred simply "moved the periods and commas around" and responded that if Donna would just let up, he would be glad to do more things with her. Donna understood what was happening like this: "He withdraws, I nag. He withdraws, I nag." Fred, however, would have characterized it this way: "She nags, I withdraw. She nags, I withdraw."

Both Fred and Donna are "punctuating" things according to linear thinking, in which there is a single cause and a single result. We might diagram it like this:

Donna nags ——————▶ Fred withdraws

Cause   Effect

Or, to look at it from the other perspective:

Fred withdraws ——————▶ Donna nags

Cause   Effect

Can you see that this way of thinking will lead nowhere? Fred and Donna will go through life sounding like a pair of broken records: "He started it!" "Well, she made me!"

Relationships, as we have seen, are interactive in nature and require that we think in terms of what are called "feedback loops." Once we understand that we are dealing with a feedback loop, however, our diagram looks more like this:

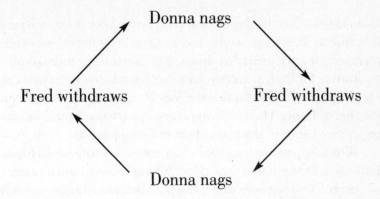

The value of seeing things this way is that it makes clear that *either* party can change the situation by changing his or her own behavior. Donna once thought nothing could change in her marriage until Fred decided to be different. But she discovered that she could impact their relationship positively by taking certain actions herself. She did not have to "just wait" for Fred. (Of course, the very same principle would apply from Fred's point of view.)

The case of Donna and Fred is a fairly simplistic one. It involves only two people and has a quick, happy ending. Most family systems are far more complex and unpredictable, and the outcomes are not usually so tidy. Still, the story of Donna and Fred really did happen, and the reason it happened the way it did is because Donna learned to see her situation as one component of a system. She learned how to think in interactive terms rather than in straight-line terms.

Let's look at a slightly more complex example. Joey is five years old. He has developed a pattern of throwing temper tantrums at bedtime. Joey's parents represent a fairly typical relational pattern. His father is away from home much of the time but is expected to be in charge when he *is* around. His mother is left to cope as best she can, with the result that she is the one who is on the scene most of the time, but without real authority to manage things.

A typical evening finds Dad lost in some television program, while Mom finishes the dinner dishes and begins the nightly process of getting Joey to bed. Joey, being a typically ingenious

five-year-old, has developed at least a dozen tactics for delaying
bedtime as long as possible, and the resulting ordeal generally
leaves Mom utterly frazzled. *Listening* to the bedtime ordeal is also
frustrating for Dad, who eventually decides that enough is enough.
He jumps out of his chair, grabs Joey by the arm and drags him
into his bedroom. He then throws Joey's pajamas at him, tells him
to get into bed *now*, slams the door and stomps away.

When he gets back to the family room, his wife is glaring at
him. "What's the matter?" he asks. "Why are you so hard on him?"
she replies. Dad has been down this path before and knows it leads
to a dead end, so he says nothing. He just turns up the volume on
the TV and flops back down in his chair.

Mom makes a snack for Joey and takes it to his room. He en-
joys a brownie between sniffles as Mom helps him put on his pajamas. She tucks him in and lies down beside him on the bed. In a
few minutes, they are both asleep.

Dad has no desire to awaken her and run the risk of resuming
the argument, so he goes to bed by himself. For the next couple
days, Joey's mom is very cool toward his dad. But Dad acts like he
doesn't notice. He goes out of his way to be thoughtful and atten-
tive. Eventually a semblance of peacefulness is restored—at least
until the next time the sequence repeats itself.

What is really going on in this situation? Perhaps Mom is angry with Dad because, instead of helping her, he leaves her alone
with the dishes and Joey. But instead of confronting him, she tries
to stuff her feelings of irritation—which wind up getting vented
on Joey instead. Perhaps Dad has had the proverbial tough day at
the office and feels justified in sitting back and taking a break. Besides, he figures, he deals with problems all day long at the office.
Is it really asking too much for his wife to keep things under control at home so he can catch his breath?

For his part, Joey has two simple objectives: He wants to stay
up a few minutes later, and he wants a bedtime snack. By now he
has learned enough about how the family works to know how to
get what he wants: If he just resists Mom and makes enough
ruckus that Dad intervenes, then before long Mom will show up

with a peace offering to help him get over Dad's outburst. No one is consciously aware of the strategies they are pursuing, but they play them out time and time again.

Who, then, is "the problem" in this situation? Is it Joey, for being an unruly child? Is it Mom, for being disorganized and inconsistent? Is it Dad, for being quick-tempered and sharp-tongued? In one sense, the answer is, "all of the above." But in a more important sense, the problem here goes beyond the behavior of any of the three individuals *as individuals*. There is a system here—an established pattern of roles and expectations as thoroughly scripted as any stage play. Until that system is addressed, the situation is unlikely ever to change.

Resistance to Change

What makes a family change? Obviously, there are many factors that impact family life in a way that prompts a family to become different. Some of these factors have to do with the normal progression of family life itself. There are a number of natural turning points in any family's history: the birth of the first child, and then of each subsequent child; the day the oldest child starts school, and the day the youngest child finishes school; children leaving home; the parents reaching retirement age; the death of one of the parents. Each of these developments (and many others besides) alters the environment in which the family lives and prompts the family to adapt—prompts it to change—in view of the new situation.

Notice how many of these turning points have to do with the addition or subtraction of family members. Family members can be added in other ways—for example, when an elderly grandparent comes to live with the family. And they can be subtracted in other ways as well, such as through divorce. Whether a given change is seen as positive or negative in itself is not the issue. It is still a stress point, something the family needs to respond to. The ease with which a family adapts to a changing environment is one of the key indicators of its healthiness or dysfunction.

Simply progressing through the life cycle gives a family ample opportunities to change. But family systems, like most systems, tend to be resistant to change. There is a kind of inertia to them, which makes them tend to keep going the way they have always gone. They have a remarkable ability to withstand and adjust to outside pressures.

This tendency of systems to continue along the same path is called *homeostasis*, which simply means "the same status." Our own bodies demonstrate how homeostasis works. Normal body temperature for most humans is 98.6 degrees. If we suddenly walk into a very warm room, our body immediately adjusts. It activates a variety of cooling systems to keep our body temperature stable. Similarly, if we walk into a cold room, our body adjusts in the opposite direction. It is designed to maintain an even 98.6 degree body temperature, no matter what the external temperature is.

Family systems work much the same way. A pattern of relationships gets established, in which everyone is assigned a role. Powerful forces within the system will work to keep things the same, even as circumstances change.

The shame-bound family system is fixed in its form and highly resistant to change, even though change is a natural fact of life. This system is analogous to peanut brittle, with each person fixed in stereotyped, inflexible roles and relationships to one another. . . . When change exerts enough force all at one moment upon a rigid system, it may break and splinter. The shame-bound system does not have good capacity to absorb very much stress and still retain its integrity.

MERLE A. FOSSUM AND MARILYN MASON, *FACING SHAME: FAMILIES IN RECOVERY*[3]

One of the most striking examples I saw of this was Clara's family. When Clara reached college age, life in her family was very tense. For a variety of reasons, Clara had always been the "glue" that held everything together. So the prospect of her departure threatened the family's very existence. Even though she had always wanted to go away to school, Clara persuaded herself that a local community college offered everything she really needed. She lived at home and got a part-time job, which helped alleviate some of the family's financial stress.

No one ever came right out and said, "Clara, you can't go. We need you here. You have to cancel your plans and stay at home." The fact was that no one needed to say anything. The message came through in hundreds of subtle, but powerful, ways. For example, when Clara was 22, she applied and was accepted to a university several hundred miles from home. She was even offered a scholarship that would have eliminated any financial obstacle. But that same year her brother graduated from high school, and even with Clara's scholarship there was no way the family could afford to put two children through college. So Clara stayed home. There was never any discussion about it; that was just the way everyone knew it needed to be.

Clara is now 36. She never did go to college, even though she helped pay for both her brother's and her younger sister's education. She still lives at home with her parents, where she continues to serve as a buffer between them. Clara knows she has missed out on a lot, and she confesses to some occasional bitterness and resentment. But she nevertheless insists that she just *couldn't* leave. Her family needed her too much. This is a remarkable example of a family system withstanding enormous outside pressure to change—in this case, the perfectly normal leaving-home stage of an oldest daughter—and managing to stay just as it always had been.

What would it take to make Clara's story come out differently? Couldn't Clara simply recognize what was happening to her and decide to take a different course? As a matter of fact, many of Clara's friends expended a great deal of energy trying to get her to do just that. Over and over again they told her she was wasting her life; that she was letting life pass her by; that she would regret it someday when her parents were gone; and so on. It was all to no avail. It's not that Clara didn't recognize the truth of what her friends were saying. As they talked, she would nod her head and say, over and over again, "Yes, yes . . . but . . ." And nothing ever changed. Clara's friends were applying linear thinking to her situation, when what was needed was interactive thinking—the recognition that it was the system, not just an individual, that needed to be addressed.

Think for a moment about how a thermostat works in your home. Let's say it is set at 70 degrees. If the temperature outside falls and the house starts to get cold, the thermostat sends a signal to the furnace to turn up the heat. If the temperature outside rises and the house starts to get too warm, the thermostat sends a signal to the air conditioner to start sending cool air through the system. Either way, the inside temperature is maintained at 70 degrees.

Now let's say the thermostat is set at 85 degrees—and let's say further that it is kept behind a locked panel so that it cannot be changed. Even in winter, 85 degrees is too warm. Since we cannot adjust the thermostat, we decide to open the window and let in some cold air. What will happen? The more cold air we let in, the more the furnace will blow hot air in its attempt to get the temperature back to 85 degrees.

In Clara's family, it is as though the thermostat is set at 85 degrees. When her friends try to get her to behave differently, it is like trying to cool the house by opening a window. Other parts of the system just work that much harder to keep things the way they were. The only way to make a lasting change in the situation is to adjust the thermostat. And the only way to do *that* is to unlock the panel that stands between the thermostat and us.

In Clara's situation, it means learning enough about Clara's family system to understand the root causes of why it is the way it is. Only then can they re-set the system. Once again, it is the system, not just the individuals, that we must look at. So, what are the forces in the system that keep families locked in dysfunctional patterns?

One major factor is simple inertia—the tendency for actions and reactions, emotions and behaviors to stay the same. Even when a need for change is acknowledged, established roles and patterns can be as hard to break as any stubborn habit. Not only does each individual family member tend to stay the same, but the different members also *reinforce* one another in their customary roles, attitudes and behaviors. It is hard to become different when everything around you is working to keep you the same.

Of course, we do not always recognize the need for change. This inability, or, in some cases, refusal to acknowledge that a problem exists, will keep us from even considering the possibility of change. There are two main things that keep us blind to the existence of problems and the need for change.

Family Secrets

One factor is that families typically have secrets. Family secrets are the things that have happened—and may still be happening—that *everyone knows about but no one ever talks about.*

As you look back at the various families we have met so far, it is easy, in most cases, to see what the family secrets were. Perhaps as you think back through your own life, you are aware of certain incidents, people or problems that no one ever discussed, even though it was obvious that everyone was aware of them. Perhaps you can recognize the part you played in maintaining the conspiracy of silence.

That conspiracy was a significant factor in Richard's family. Richard came for therapy with a great amount of reluctance. He was almost overwhelmed by the feeling that he was betraying his family members by talking about their problems to an outsider. "We were taught from an early age that family business stays in the family," he explained.

The main item of "family business," as it turned out, was Richard's father, who suffered periodic mental breakdowns. As Richard poured out his history, he told about the times when his father would "flip out." Among the most terrifying memories were the times when his father would load the children in the car and drive crazily around town for hours at a time.

After such an episode, Richard's mother would manage to get her husband into a hospital for treatment. While he was there, she and Richard's brothers would literally pack up and move to another part of town where no one knew them or their awful secret. By the time Richard's father got out of the hospital, the family would be relocated, and his psychotic episode would be buried in the past. Richard said this sequence of events had occurred 10 times by the time he turned 16.

Finally, Richard's father was committed to the state hospital for good. He remains there to this day. Richard and his brothers visit him regularly. They long ago settled into a rotation, in which a different brother goes to visit each week. Interestingly, they manage to do this without ever discussing it. Richard simply takes his turn every six weeks. He has been doing this faithfully for 20 years.

During all those years, whenever Richard's family has gotten together, Dad has emphatically not been a topic of conversation. No one has ever commented on how they thought Dad was doing. No one has ever talked about how it felt to have a father in a psychiatric institution. No one has ever talked about how it felt to have to pull up stakes and move every time Dad had an episode.

Sometimes family secrets are buried even more deeply than Richard's. One day in her therapy group, Marge told how she had just learned two years before that her father was an alcoholic. Someone asked how long he had been drinking. "Oh, all my life," Marge said. "In fact, he was an active alcoholic even before I was born." Marge was 41 years old when she shared this. That meant she had lived for 39 years with a practicing alcoholic—without even realizing it.

The rest of the group looked at her in disbelief. How could she not have known that her own father was an alcoholic? "It was a secret," Marge said with a shrug. "Somehow, Mom managed to keep it hidden. And not just from us kids, either. No one in the family knew. No one in town knew. They just thought he was sick a lot." Marge noted that a lot of her father's "illnesses," which had puzzled her at the time, finally began to make sense once she understood her father's real problem. She had wondered about those illnesses while she was growing up. But she knew that Dad's health was a closed subject, something you simply did not ask about.

Family secrets are like having an elephant in the parlor. You learn at a very young age that the one question you *never* ask is, "Why do we have an elephant in the parlor?" If friends or others outside ask about it, the correct answer is, "What elephant?" As the elephant grows, you put a lamp and a lace doily on it and treat it like part of the furniture. In time you have to avoid the parlor entirely. But you never ask about it or comment on it. And a friend also doesn't ask, when he visits, "Why do you have an elephant in your living room?" because he doesn't want you to ask when you visit his home, "Why do you have a dead dog in your living room?"

> *What is common to all such families is the commitment of all family members to maintain the secrets through rigid rules about what may and may not be talked about. These rules prohibit spontaneity in the family relationships; with spontaneity the real feelings and facts might be revealed. Family members create powerful myths about their histories, often leaving out the painful historical shapers of the shame. The children in these families are loyal through their lack of questioning about the past, thereby colluding in the family's rules.*
>
> MERLE A. FOSSUM AND MARILYN MASON,
> *FACING SHAME: FAMILIES IN RECOVERY*[4]

Family secrets are one of the main ways that family systems resist change. Everyone keeps doing what he or she has always done, as if nothing were wrong. Richard found that in order to break out of his family's dysfunctional system, he had to start talking about his dad. In the same way, Marge knew that she needed to learn more about alcoholism and about how her dad's drinking had impacted her during her formative years.

Family Myths

The opposite of family secrets are family myths. Myths are the *things we talk about but never do*. George Bernard Shaw once said that most history was nothing more than "a lie agreed upon." Family myths are like that. They represent a silent conspiracy to pretend that things are different than they are. Ask almost anyone about his or her family, and the first thing you are likely to hear is one of the family's myths.

The most common of these, perhaps, is the one that says, "Oh, our family was very close." Time and again, when I have asked people to tell me about their family, the first words out of their mouth will be, "Well, you know, we're a very close family." Then they go on to tell me about all the problems, hurts and disappointments their family has caused them, describing anything but closeness and warmth. But as they finish their account, they invariably conclude by saying, "But our family is really close."

There are other common myths. People will say that their family was very loving or caring. People from strong religious backgrounds will often say that their family was very spiritual, even when there is little evidence of it.

Not surprisingly, family myths are frequently connected to family secrets: The one thing the family is most ashamed of will be the thing they try to cover over with a myth. I remember Anne telling me about her family when she came in to the hospital. In between the various problems she described, she mentioned repeatedly that her family was "very supportive." "We're always there for each other," she would say. But about two weeks later, she exploded. "I thought my family was supportive. But here I've been in the hospital for two weeks, and not a single one of them has come to see me. They haven't even called. It's like they don't want to admit I'm here."

The realization that she was living a myth—painful as it was—turned out to be a key to Anne's recovery. Myths are powerful forces that help dysfunctional families stay locked in their unhealthy patterns. Until they confront them and uncover the reality behind them, everything continues to stay the same.

Where do family myths come from? To some degree, they are simply a social convention, as when someone asks, "How are you doing?" and you answer, "Fine, thanks." But there is more to it than that. We have all been programmed in various ways as to what a "normal" or "happy" family is like. It is like the families we used to see on television programs, or read about in schoolbooks growing up. We know what a family is *supposed* to be like, and we have a natural reluctance to acknowledge that our family was not like that. Never mind that the images we have in our mind may be absurdly unrealistic. We want to believe that they are true, and that our life compares well with them. To acknowledge otherwise—to others and even to ourselves—would be too painful. Let's look now at why our expectations for family don't measure up to what we experience.

KEY POINTS TO REMEMBER

1. Family works as a system.

2. Individual problems are often best understood in the context of the family system.

3. Systems are resistant to change, especially unhealthy family systems.

4. The family is more than the number of people connected—it is a powerful system.

5. To better understand ourselves and our family, we need to think interactively.

6. Trying harder only gets you more of the same.

7. We need to look at how we "punctuate" an event, or a series of events.

8. Family secrets and family myths help maintain status quo in the family.

Notes

1. Robert Hemfelt and Paul Warren, *Kids Who Carry Our Pain* (Nashville, TN: Thomas Nelson Publishers, 1990), p. 70.

2. Lynn Hoffman, *Foundations of Family Therapy* (New York: Basic Books, 1981), p. 31.

3. Merle A. Fossum and Marilyn Mason, *Facing Shame: Families in Recovery* (New York: W.W. Norton, 1986), p. 19.

4. Ibid., pp. 45-46.

My Family and Me

*All families are imperfect. But some families are
healthier than others. How can you measure the
ways in which your own family fell short of the ideal,
to better understand your own need for healing?*

Just what *is* a normal family anyway? In chapter 1, I explained
the family in its most basic form, with an emphasis on *parenting*
that expresses itself in an *unconditional love* that allows for the development of an *autonomously attached adult*. In this chapter, I will
spell out in greater detail what I mean when I talk about a normal, or healthy, family. We will look at some of the more common deviations from this norm and identify some of the
varieties of unhealthy families that result. Then, in later chapters, you will learn some tools and techniques that will help you
apply this analysis to your own situation.

The Well-Adjusted Family

Many psychologists and counselors have tried to outline the characteristics of a healthy family. One writer has developed a description of what he calls the "well-adjusted" family.[1] He speaks of a
balance between "autonomy" and "attachment" in which there is
a minimum of *fusion* between people and, at the same time, a minimum of *distance* between them. He also speaks of a balance between *individual* and *family* needs, and of an adaptability that
enables the family to adjust to changing needs and circumstances.

One of the key indicators we will identify of a well-adjusted family is that *problems are seen as family problems, not just as individual problems*. In other words, there is a sense that "We're all in this together, and we're *for* each other in whatever problems arise. If *you* have a problem, then *we* have a problem." At the same time, there is a healthy insistence that individuals take responsibility for their own lives, and people deal with one another straightforwardly and directly, rather than through third parties or go-betweens.

Indeed, within the context of a common set of basic values, individual differences are not only tolerated, they are encouraged—even celebrated. People who grow up in such a family can interact well with others and accept a variety of expressions of opinions, attitudes and emotions.

A second indicator of a well-adjusted family is that it demonstrates *a respect for members of other generations*. The young do not isolate themselves from the old, nor do the old cut themselves off from the children and young adults. People are connected with their parents; they recognize and appreciate the benefits they derive from one another, as well as the benefits they can provide for one another. Other family members are not seen as emotional crutches to be used or leaned on, but as resources for learning and growth, for feedback and enjoyment.

A third indicator in a well-adjusted family is that *people are free to "experience their own emptiness."*[2] All of us experience good times and bad times, times when we are up and times when we are down. It is especially in the down times that we usually feel most unaccepted by others. In the well-adjusted family, people are given the space to experience and express even the down side of their emotions without others attempting to judge them or "fix" them, or encouraging them to repress their feelings. In short, the well-adjusted family has found a balance between two seemingly contradictory dynamics: being close and being separate. These dynamics must be balanced within each of us if we are to be healthy as individuals; they must also be balanced in our families.

For a family to experience these three indicators, there needs to be a solid foundation built to define how its members connect with each other. These connections are formed in the early years of our experience and set in motion patterns that carry on throughout our lives, unless there is some intervention that takes place along the way. Not everyone needs an intervention, for some of us were fortunate to be raised in a family in which we learned to experience healthy connections with other people. God has wired every human being for connection, but He has left it to our families to determine how secure our wiring is in place. Let's look first at what a healthy connection looks like.

A Secure Attachment

How we work through the opposing movements required in our family has its roots in our early development. I can illustrate this point through the birth of one of my grandchildren. When Jonathan was in the womb, he was in a perfect environment. All of his needs were met before he even experienced them. The womb was a quiet, safe world for him. Then came birth, and it was like Adam and Eve being expelled from the Garden of Eden. He left that perfect world to enter a very imperfect world.

My wife and I got to see Jonathan soon after he was born. His parents had held him for a while, and then the nurse took him to the nursery where they would clean him up. On the way to the nursery, she brought Jonathan by the room we were in, and we got to admire him but didn't hold him. He was still covered with the birth fluids and needed to be cleaned up. After we got a few minutes to check him out, the nurse took him into the nursery and put him on a special table to do the cleaning task. Well, first they turned on bright lights so they could really see him. Remember, he had been in darkness for nine months, and the lights must have been blindingly bright to him. Then they started to scrape him clean. I know they were very gentle, but nothing had ever touched his skin before. After he was clean, they stretched him so they could measure him, then they weighed him and took footprints. Finally they put some stuff in his eyes, wrapped him up, and put him in a bassinet where we could watch him fall asleep. What a welcome into this new world!

But the "welcome" wasn't finished. A few hours later, Jonathan woke up crying. He was experiencing his first need: hunger! And because he didn't know how to eat, and his mother didn't know how to breastfeed him, it was a laborious process. Eventually a coach came to help his mother teach him how to eat. But finally, on this first attempt, his hunger was satisfied and he fell back asleep. And eventually, he had another new experience—what went into his stomach had to come out the other end.

It became quite easy to see that Jonathan's first task of living in this strange new world was to find some way to make it feel safe. If his dad and, especially, his mom form a secure attachment with Jonathan, then he will feel safe, and it will have a positive effect on all of his relationships throughout his life.

Sir John Bowlby was an early voice in articulating the importance of the secure attachment between a mother and her infant. He described it as the child having "a secure base" from which he or she could leave to go out and explore the world, and when it started to feel unsafe, he or she could retreat back to the secure base—which was the relationship with the mother. In some ways, this secure base could be likened to a fortress or castle. The more secure the child is in the fortress, the more comfortable he is in leaving the fortress and exploring the surrounding woods.

The secure attachment requires three things from the mother in relation to the child. First, she needs to be available. When the child needs something from the mother, she needs to be where the child can find her. If mom is talking with a friend, or on the phone, it doesn't mean the child has the right to interrupt; but in a healthy situation like that, the mother will acknowledge the child's need in some way, delaying her response until she has finished. The unavailable mother is the one who is too busy, or too self-occupied, to even notice the child needs something.

Second, she needs to be responsive to the child. If she isn't available, how can she be responsive? So she has to be where the child can find her, and then she needs to respond to what the child needs. The mother who is on the phone and ignores the child is being unresponsive.

Third, she needs to be accepting of the child. Feeling accepted is so critical in the child's development of a secure attachment. This doesn't mean the mother can't discipline the child or express frustration with the child's behavior. It really is about communicating to the child the ongoing sense of unconditional love and acceptance in the midst of discipline or correction. These are the three components of a secure attachment, and the pattern is usually set by the end of the first year of a child's life.

Obviously, the parent can't be perfect in how she does these three things. In fact, perfection on the part of the parent leads to other attachment issues. The mother who is overboard on how she does these three things will give the child a feeling of entitlement and grandiosity, and he or she will become very demanding of everyone, especially the parents. No, the mother only needs to be "good enough" in being available, responsive and accepting. And the "good enough" parenting will be reflected in the child not feeling cheated in any of these three areas.

Bowlby described one example of a secure attachment between the mother and the child. When he went to the park to watch mothers with their toddlers, he noticed the toddler who would go off and play with the other children, and every so often, the child would return to the mother for a reassuring hug or touch, or even just to make eye contact with the mother. It's like the child left the secure base—mother—and was out exploring and enjoying life. Then when he or she started to feel a little insecure, he or she would reconnect with the base—the mother—and be reassured and then return to playing with the other kids.

Another example was a research project called the "strange situation." Here, after the mother-child relationship had been observed in the home, the mother and the child would be brought to the research center and invited to enter a room filled with toys. The child would of course begin to play with the toys. A short time later, a stranger would enter the room and silently sit down. The child with the secure attachment would notice the stranger, make some contact with the mother and then return to playing. A short time later, the mother would briefly leave the room. The child would stop and look, then continue playing. When the mother returned to the room, the child would go for a hug or a touch and then back to the toys.

When a child experiences a secure attachment, it forms the foundation for the second task in his or her life. Somewhere around the eighth to tenth month of Jonathan's life, he started to work on his secondary task. No longer was he content just cuddling and being loved; he wanted to leave the secure base and explore. He started to crawl, and then walk. And have you ever noticed that when children begin to crawl or walk, they are always moving away from us? After all, have you ever seen a toddler chasing his mom at the mall? No, it's always the mom chasing the toddler.

When Jonathan reached this stage, it was as if he were saying, "I've seen enough of you guys—I know you are there. I feel safe enough now to want to see more of the world." It is not fear that is at work here. One might say it is more of a natural curiosity we all are born with. It's a drive toward autonomy.

Now he doesn't want too much autonomy. He just feels safe and secure enough to venture out to explore the rest of the world. When it gets scary, he comes scurrying back to the safety of his base. I remember this vividly illustrated with Jonathan when he was about two. We were at an outdoor mall with beautiful areas filled with flowers. He was happily exploring. When it came time to leave, his mom and dad called him, but he was engrossed in what he was doing and he ignored them. He felt quite secure, obviously. Finally one of us said, "Hey, Jonathan. We're leaving. Goodbye!" He stopped short—took a second to think, and then immediately turned and ran back to his "secure base."

These two movements form the foundation for all of our relationships as adults, especially our family relationships. One movement is the desire to move toward each other, which is the movement of love. The other movement is the desire to move away, to develop or to retain some degree of autonomy or separateness. Too much closeness and we are enmeshed with each other. Too much autonomy and we are disengaged with each other. Families take on these characteristics.

When either of these two dynamics gets seriously out of balance, the result is an unhealthy family, or dysfunction. Bowlby and others have identified three insecure attachment styles that result from availability, responsiveness and acceptance being out of balance or absent in the child's experience.

Insecure Attachments

A mom, or the mothering person, is the one who is the primary creator of a safe fortress for their children, especially in the early developmental years. Dads are a part of the process, but not as central in the first year of the child's life. Children raised in a relatively stable environment that balances attaching love with healthy limits on autonomy will grow into adults who are secure in their ability to experience secure attachments. But a lot us didn't grow up in that healthy environment. Our ability to feel secure in our adult relationships is marred or broken by our attachment styles. What happens when Mom and/or Dad didn't provide a safe fortress for us in those early years? What if the fortress felt safe some of the time but not other times, or what if it never felt secure?

The outcome of insecure attachments can lead to one or some combination of three faulty forms of relating: (1) the avoidant attachment, (2) the anxious attachment, and/or (2) the fearful attachment. Let's look at each one.

The Avoidant Attachment Style

What happens when, in a family, the safe fortress a person needed wasn't safe, or the parents were completely unavailable? What happens when a parent dies or leaves during those first years of a child's life? Or when the mother and father are emotionally unavailable, overwhelmed or distant and cold? The result is that a person grows into an adult who has learned to be self-sufficient.

If our attachment style is avoidant, we've learned from an early age not to trust anyone else. We cannot depend on anyone else to take care of us—we learned to be self-sufficient. We carry this style into all of our adult relationships, especially into our marriage. We long for a close, intimate relationship, but we become uncomfortable with that closeness when we begin to experience it. Our self-sufficiency is in conflict with our need for connection, and usually the avoidant behavior wins out.

Closeness feels controlling, and control issues are big for those who experience the avoidant attachment style. Closeness also demands too much of us emotionally, so making any relational commitments, especially a marriage commitment, feels like we have to give up our independence. Trust is a big issue. We may trust little bits of ourself to selected people, but in the end, we only trust ourself. After all, that's what we've had to do from the beginning. So our efforts at closeness are always overpowered by distancing, or avoiding, behaviors.

In the situation described earlier, the toddler with a developing avoidant style noticed when the stranger entered the room, when Mom left the room and when Mom returned to the room. But no effort was made to reconnect with Mom, for after all, Mom is really not that important.

In adults, those with an avoidant attachment style are the lone rangers in our life. They seem to want connection, but they back away from it very quickly when it is available. Some don't even believe they want connection—they are happy being connected to their computer, to their job or to some other inanimate object that makes no demands on them.

The Anxious Attachment Style

What happens to a person when the safe fortress is always under repair during those early years? When he or she runs for shelter and safety only to find that one of the walls that is supposed to provide safety isn't there? What is supposed to feel safe doesn't feel safe. Perhaps Mom is sick a lot; so she may be there, but she's not there emotionally. Or Mom and Dad are always fighting and talking of divorce. Children in these situations often seek reassurance that everything is going to be okay. They become clingy and need more emotional support than they can get.

Fear of abandonment is a major theme in their relationships. As adults, those with an anxious attachment style often seek to become one with their close friends, and especially with a spouse. If they could just be "joined at the hip" they believe they would finally feel secure—a spouse or close friend will never leave. But at the same time, they struggle with feeling flawed deep down inside and unworthy of being loved. In their anxiety about being abandoned, they do what you would least expect—they are critical of the other person to the point they almost drive that person away. But then, if they drive them away, they really weren't abandoned.

Those who are in relationship with the anxious attachment person often experience him or her as unpredictable—sometimes wanting almost a symbiotic closeness and then, without warning, being critical and pulling away.

Toddlers with an anxious attachment style continually seek reassurance. Remember the experiment of a mom and her child and a stranger in a room? When the stranger entered the room, the child retreated to Mom and may have acted whiny and clingy. Mom might encourage the child to go back and play with the toys, but when Mom left the room, the child panicked. The child would scream and cry, standing by the door watching for his mom to return. But when the mom returned, he might even hit his mom, expressing anger at her abandonment.

As adults, those with an anxious attachment style appear to move between desperately wanting connection and backing away from it. They use criticism as a way to sabotage the connection they long for and are beginning to experience.

The Fearful Attachment Style

The fearful attachment style is developed in a child who is afraid to run back to the supposedly safe fortress. For this child it has never really felt safe. At times it may have been safe, but those times are more than offset by the overall feeling of it being unsafe. Verbal, emotional and especially physical abuse are part of the early experience for a fearfully attached child. The desire to be attached and close is there, but fear keeps the child away from what he or she desperately wants and needs.

Children with this style typically blame themselves for the lack of safety in their fortress, and they try harder to be perfect, thinking this will cause the significant adults to make things safe. But it is all to no avail. Inside, the child feels unworthy of being loved, and fear is the basic response in his or her adult relationships. They, too, are fearful of being abandoned, for that has been a consistent experience while growing up.

Adults with a fearful attachment style often marry someone who is needier than they are, such as an addict, alcoholic or irresponsible type of individual. Of course, the result of this is a continuation of the lack of safety in relationships. As they did in childhood, they struggle to cover up abandonment issues, working harder and harder to make the relationship work and find a safe place for himself or herself.

A classic example was what happened with a fearfully attached child when the mother returned to the room. The child started toward the mother with arms outstretched, preparing to hug the mother. But halfway to the mother, he stopped, turned around and backed in to the mother. He didn't know whether he was going to get a hug or get smacked for something.

Of course, each of these insecure attachment styles helps create different family styles. Let's look briefly at how these insecure attachments fit into some of the common types of dysfunctional families.

Common Types of Unhealthy Family Patterns

In my work with families, sometimes people wonder how anyone can understand the chaos. You may be thinking that ultimately there are as many types of unhealthy families as there are families. But it may surprise you to learn that there are some common varieties of unhealthy families, and they are fewer than the many varieties of healthy families. Every healthy family system is unique and varied, perhaps because they have a greater degree of flexibility; whereas in unhealthy families, rigidity and resistance to change allow for common patterns that are more easily identified.

Though every situation is unique, most unhealthy families will fall into one of several recognizable categories.[3] If you came from an unhealthy family system, chances are good that you will be able to identify your family type in the list that follows. These common types of unhealthy family patterns are based on problems in the attachment process. The three less-secure attachment styles identified by Bowlby and others would lead us to one of these common types of family systems.

Isolated Islands

In some ways, this kind of family bears scarcely any resemblance to a "family" at all, because the individual members are so isolated from one another. They are like some of the island groups in the South Pacific. If you were to view them from a great distance, or if you were to photograph them from a satellite in outer space, you would be able to recognize that they do in fact go together in some way. But if you were actually standing on one of them, you would think you were all alone in the middle of the ocean. The other islands in the group would be so distant you would not be able to see them over the horizon.

The predominate attachment style in these families is the avoidant style. Because the members share the same last name and address, it is possible to see that they go together. But in terms of the internal dynamics of family life, they are almost totally detached from one another. They are isolated islands living in the same place.

This is probably the most severely disturbed pattern of family dysfunction and the one that has the most negative impact on its members. People from this kind of family are like isolated islands, with few (if any) personal relationships that involve any degree of attachment. Whatever relationships they *do* have are typically devoid of emotional content, existing for utilitarian purposes only.

Let's go back again to Larry, who was emotionally deserted by his parents long before they literally abandoned him at age five, leaving him in the care of his aunt and uncle. His new family was not much different from his old one. Larry would be quick to point out that his aunt and uncle "took good care of him," that they gave him a warm bed to sleep in and three square meals a day. But emotionally, Larry was raised in a vacuum.

Deep inside, Larry longed for emotional closeness—to connect with someone. But those longings stayed deep inside. Bringing them to the surface, let alone acting on them, was far too frightening a prospect, even with his wife and children. It was not until his depression deepened to the point of threatening his life that Larry could bring himself to take the terrifying step of reaching out to others—to start building bridges from his isolated island to the world around him.

Generational Splits

The distinguishing characteristic of this kind of family is a lack of significant interaction between parents and children—not just the two generations currently living in the same household, but also between Mom and Dad and *their* parents. Significant interaction takes place only within generations. This also is generated predominately by the avoidant attachment style or the anxious attachment style.

Interestingly, a frequent pattern in this type of family is for emotional and relational connections to *skip*, or leapfrog, generations. For example, the children in a particular family may be isolated from their parents but experience a high degree of emotional warmth and nurture from one or both sets of grandparents. When these children themselves grow up and raise a family, their own parents—who largely neglected them—will take a strong interest in the grandchildren. And so it goes, generation after generation.

Rick and Beth provide an example. They had three daughters. But they had remarkably little involvement with them. They were very much involved with one another, however. They worked together in real estate and took vacations together—without the kids. As a result, their daughters became very close. Outsiders looked at them with admiration; they were so tight-knit, so supportive, so loving. What those outside observers did not realize was that the girls would have loved for their lives to be different, but they had no choice; there was no one else for them to turn to but each other. When the girls were little, Beth's parents stayed with them a lot. After Beth's parents died, a variety of Rick's and Beth's friends filled in until the girls were old enough to care for themselves without a sitter.

Now, years later, all three of the girls are married. Rick and Beth have four grandchildren and more on the way. Rick and Beth are virtually obsessed with their grandchildren. They have dozens of pictures of them on the walls of their home and offices. Beth doesn't work much anymore—she spends a lot of time watching the babies. When she and Rick go on vacations now, they often take the older grandchildren along with them. As for the three daughters, they are too busy with their husbands and careers to spend much time with their kids. The unhealthy pattern continues.

Gender Splits

This is similar to the generational split except that the split happens along gender lines within families. The men and boys stick together, as do the women and girls. The whole family spends time together and does things together, of course, but very little emotionally significant interaction takes place across gender lines. There may be an anxious attachment style behind this, but also a fearful attachment style could explain the gender split.

Much of the time this pattern is found in families with a very strong notion of sex-based roles for men and women. Not just that there is "men's work" and "women's work," but that there is a "man's world" and a "woman's world." Women have "their place"—usually in the kitchen—and the girls are expected to be there with them. The men have more choices where they go together. (They usually stay away from the kitchen, though, since that is where the women are.)

My own family was a lot like this while I was growing up. Even when we sat down to eat at the kitchen table, my dad and I sat on one side of the table, and my mother and sister sat on the other side. When we went somewhere in the car, the men sat in the front seat and the women sat in the back.

There is a great deal of evidence that children benefit from a strong identification with the same-sex parent. It is especially important for developing a clear gender identity and sexual orientation. But children also need appropriate exposure to their opposite-sex parent and siblings. If they do not get it, they can grow up fearful or disdainful of one another.

The Fused Pair

In this type of family, two members of the family are cut off—or rather, they cut themselves off—from the others. This fused pair becomes the nucleus around which the rest of the family revolves. The anxious attachment style may be at work here when two needy members of the family become "glued to each other's hip."

Marti, the woman we met earlier in this chapter, came from a family like this. In her case, it was Marti and her mother who became fused together while Marti was growing up. Early on, her mother had dismissed her father as a significant factor in the family because of a "moral lapse" on his part. From then on, her mother invested everything in Marti in an apparent effort to draw from her relationship with her daughter what was not available to her anywhere else. She paid as little attention as possible to Marti's father and Marti's other two sisters. Being fused with her mother in this way produced Marti's mixed feelings toward her mother: bitterness mixed with reluctance to be "disloyal."

In this kind of system, the other members experience the family as extremely disengaged and detached, much like those who grow up in a family of "isolated islands." But the two people who are fused experience the family as being strongly enmeshed. This type of family manages the extraordinary task of occupying both ends of the attachment scale at the same time.

Queen of the Hill

This is a family completely dominated by one person. It could be anyone, but in the vast majority of cases it is the mother. There is no mistaking where the power lies and who is in charge. Everything must go through Mother. If anyone needs anything, they get it from her; if they want to do anything, they must clear it with her. If they have a problem, they take it to Mother—and nowhere else.

In some extended families, Grandmother is the reigning matriarch. In these cases, Mom is just as subservient as everyone else, but she knows the day will come when she ascends the throne. She is simply waiting her turn.

Mary—the girl in chapter 1 who was raped by her older brother when she was young—came from this kind of family. Even though Mary's mother was gone from the home a great deal, there was no questioning the fact that she was in charge. Mary's father was just as powerless as the children. When Mary tried to tell what her brother had done, and her mother refused to believe her, that was the end of the discussion. No one questioned her mom's decision.

The Quiet Dictator

This type of family is similar in some respects to the one dominated by a "Queen of the Hill"; however, in this case the dominant member's control over the family is far more subtle and manipulative in nature. A "Queen of the Hill" type tends to be very upfront and imperious in her domination of the family, while a "Quiet Dictator" works behind the scenes, pulling the strings quietly and unobtrusively, skillfully manipulating others' emotions.

To the skilled eye, the Quiet Dictator is not hard to identify. Usually this is the one person who refuses to participate in counseling—or if he/she does show up, the person either tries to sidetrack the conversation or simply refuses to talk altogether. When a sensitive topic is raised, the eyes of the other family members inadvertently turn to this individual for cues as to what to do next.

There are clear, ironclad rules and expectations, enforced by a firm set of roles that the members are to fulfill without wavering. This dynamic is probably based on the avoidant attachment style, as there is very little real connection in this type of family.

The Family Scapegoat

We have already mentioned the tendency for families to make one member serve as a scapegoat—someone who bears the blame for the family's problems. The scapegoat image is drawn from the Bible. In the Old Testament, when the Jewish people wanted to be reconciled to God, they would symbolically place their sin on a goat that had been specially chosen for the occasion. The goat would then either be sacrificed or sent away, never to return.

As you can imagine, being a scapegoat is not a happy experience. I remember when Eddie came into the hospital. When we talked to him about inviting his family for Family Day, he hesitated, and asked if he really had to. We asked what his concerns were. "They're all against me," he said. "They treat me like an outsider."

Nevertheless, when Family Day rolled around two weeks later, Eddie had his whole family there. Everything seemed perfectly normal—for a while. Then one of our counselors began leading a discussion group designed to draw out what various family members were thinking and feeling below the surface. It was Eddie's sister who finally blurted out that Eddie "just never fit in." The rest of the family "does just great together," she said. "But whenever Eddie's around, there's tension." She sat back with a relieved look on her face, as though relieved that a dark secret was finally out in the open.

The more our counselor probed with the family, it became increasingly clear that Eddie had been treated as a classic family scapegoat. When you talked with Eddie by himself, he was a pleasant, normal person. When you talked with his family, they too seemed like pleasant, normal people. But when you put them together, it did not take long to see that what looked good on the surface was, in reality, anything but that. There were serious tensions, and Eddie, in the mind of everyone else, was to blame for all of them. Inevitably, he had begun to accept this assessment of the situation and played his assigned role perfectly.

So far our discussion about normal and dysfunctional families has been at the level of "concepts" and "dynamics" and "general theories." But what about *your* family? How did *it* operate? What were its unique strengths and weaknesses? How did these qualities affect *you*? In the next chapters, we will learn how to use some tools that can begin to help you better understand your own family system and its unique issues.

KEY POINTS TO REMEMBER

1. Healthy families have a sense of working together as a system.

2. The more secure the attachments between people in the family, the healthier the family and the individuals in that family.

3. Secure attachments are based on availability, responsiveness and acceptance.

4. Unhealthy attachments are either avoidant, anxious/ambivalent or fearful.

5. Unhealthy families form predictable patterns—healthy families are multi-variable.

Notes

1. T. F. Fogerty, "Systems Concepts and the Dimensions of Self," quoted in P. J. Guerin, ed., *Family Therapy: Theory and Practice* (New York: Gardner Press, 1976).
2. Ibid.
3. The particular set of categories comes from H. Peter Laqueur, "Multiple Family Therapy," cited in Guerin, *Family Therapy: Theory and Practice*.

The Sins of the Fathers

There is nothing new under the sun.
The problems your family experience frequently
have their roots in patterns of dysfunction that are
handed down from generation to generation.
A simple tool called a genogram can help you
better understand a heritage of dysfunction.

For a number of years, I have been teaching a class at Fuller Theological Seminary titled "Family Therapy and Pastoral Care." On paper, it looks like a snap course. There is a lot of reading, but there are no exams and no research papers due. The only project a student has to create is a four-generational genogram of his or her family, and if married, the family of his or her spouse. When students sign up for the class, I'm not sure how many of them even know what a genogram is. But by the time they complete the course, they not only know what it is, but they also have been able to see the incredible value a genogram provides in understanding themselves and their family.

One student reported finding out that her family had a big secret. Her father had been married before. This student was in her late thirties and had no idea that her father had had a previous marriage. She found out when she asked questions of a relative the family had described as the "black sheep" in the family. I've found that many people are labeled the black sheep of the family because they are "truth-tellers," and this relative was that indeed.

But that wasn't all—there was a child in that secret marriage. For almost 40 years, this person had a half-sibling she had never even heard about. But there was more. She found out that not only had her father done this, but also his father had done the same thing!

The genogram is one of the most helpful tools a person can use to understand the dynamics of his or her family system. It is a sort of expanded family tree that charts the relational and emotional aspects of a family across several generations. It includes the kind of information that a typical family tree would contain—names, birthdays, weddings, divorces, deaths and the like. But it also includes brief descriptions of family members, their particular strengths and weaknesses, aspects of their lives that can have a continuing effect through the years, as well as the types of relationships each had with the other members of the family. It is put together in a way that makes it possible to identity principles and patterns that have been at work across the generations.

If you have thumbed ahead in this chapter and have seen what a genogram looks like, you may feel a bit intimidated by it. Let me simply assure you before we go any further that a genogram is not as complicated as it appears to be. The various symbols may be new to you, but they are not hard to understand. And when you are working with a genogram of your own family—as hopefully you will be by the time we have finished this chapter—the fact that you are working with familiar names and events will make it easier for you.

> *The first step in releasing the past is to become*
> *aware of the problems that still exist. Identify what it*
> *is from your past that still bothers you, affects you,*
> *influences you or hinders you.*
> H. NORMAN WRIGHT, *ALWAYS DADDY'S GIRL*[1]

Before we get into the "how" of constructing a genogram, let's talk for a moment about the "why." There are three main benefits we can gain from the use of the genogram.

- The first is *understanding*. As you develop your genogram, you will be able to see and understand your family as more than just a collection of individuals. You will be able to see it as a unified whole, as a system. You will be able to identity patterns and tendencies that may have characterized your family for years, and that impact you to this day. This enhanced understanding will apply not only to your family as a whole, but also to specific generations of the family and even to particular individuals.

- As understanding increases, so does the *potential for change*. It is nearly impossible to change something we do not see or understand. But once we can recognize where problems and weaknesses lie, the potential for changing them becomes available to us.

- This brings us to the third benefit that genograms provide help with, which represents the whole point of this book. Once we start to understand the dynamics at work in our family system, and begin to grasp the potential for change, we are able to consider the crucial step we must take if we are to find freedom from the effects of the past. That step is *forgiveness*.

===

*If we can move toward gathering a more
factual history of our family, and enlarge the context
over several generations, we will gain a more
objective perspective on family members. We can
begin to see our parents, as well as other relatives,
as real people in context who have both strengths
and vulnerabilities—as all human beings do.
And if we can learn to be more objective in our own
family, other relationships will be a piece of cake.*

HARRIET LERNER, *THE DANCE OF INTIMACY*[2]

===

Drawing the Boundaries

Now let's look at some of the family dynamics that can be clarified through the use of the genogram. The first is the dynamic of *boundaries*. One of the best descriptions we have read of how boundaries work within a family system comes from the book *Adult Children*:

> We are talking about psychological and social boundaries here, although in principle they are the same as physical boundaries around one's property, city, state or country. For our purposes we will look at three types of boundaries:
>
> 1. Individual boundaries: Our personal boundaries, which define who we are in relationship to others.
>
> 2. Intergenerational boundaries: Boundaries that help us define who the parents and children are, for example. When these boundaries are blurred, the children often become the parent to the parent.
>
> 3. Family boundaries: Boundaries that define our family and make it distinctive from other families.
>
> Within each type, we can have three boundary states:
>
> 1. Rigid boundaries, which are too strong, can be likened to walls without doors. They are often impenetrable. We cannot move back and forth across the boundary.
>
> 2. Diffuse boundaries, which are too weak, can be likened to defining our property by drawing a line in the dirt with a stick. It does not take much to wipe out the boundary. People with diffuse boundaries may say no to something, but they change their minds with a little encouragement.

3. Flexible boundaries, which are healthy, can bend
   when they need to. If the circumstances warrant
   it, the no can be changed to yes, but never out of
   guilt or a sense of being forced into something.
   Flexible boundaries allow the other person to
   say no. The person who asked is then able to accept the no and find another way to accomplish
   the task.[3]

The way boundaries worked in your family has a lot to do with how you relate to your world today. A genogram will help you identify the types of boundaries that existed (and still exist) in your family and the way they may have affected you for good or for ill.

The Roles We Play

A second dynamic identified with a genogram is that of *roles* and how they are played out. A role is simply any fixed pattern of relating that forces us into set actions, behaviors and responses. These are done out of habit rather than as a freely chosen response to changing circumstances and situations. When roles work like this, they dehumanize us. People do not relate to us as full, free human beings with individual dignity and free will, but only in terms of our role. We are treated not as "Dave" or "Joan" but as "the Black Sheep," "the Scapegoat," "the Kid Brother," and so on.

I have already described some of the more common family roles—like the Scapegoat—that occur with some frequency in many families. But ultimately, there are as many different roles as there are individuals within families. The point is not to draw up a comprehensive list of standard family roles, but to understand the roles that have existed in our own family and how those roles have affected us:

Families cast their members in roles that they never forget. Although we may be separated, literally or figuratively,
from our families of origin, these major roles are indelibly

engraved on our memories. We replay these roles over and over again, not just in families we form but often in other groups as well. We are attracted to people who play, and let us play, the roles we know. Sometimes, we do not want the role we played as a child, and choose another role. But that role will also be familiar to us—a role that someone else played in our family of origin.[4]

Thus it is important to know what role (or roles) we played in our family, as well as the roles we play today. It is also important to understand the roles that others played, and how the roles are interconnected. Seeing the whole will enable us to better understand the particular parts.

The Rules We Follow

Every family system operates according to a set of rules, or what are known in the business world as "standard operating procedures." Rules may be spoken or unspoken. Nevertheless, they exist and they affect our family's activities and behaviors. Even without saying a word, our family lets us know what is and is not acceptable, how various circumstances are to be assessed and responded to, and how different individuals ought to act and react in different situations.

Remember Richard, from chapter 2, whose father was in a state mental hospital? Richard and his brothers took turns visiting their father every week, but they never talked about it or about him. "Visit Dad every six weeks" and "Never mention Dad's existence" were both very strong, very clear rules in Richard's family, even though they were never stated out loud.

In any family there are likely to be rules to control such areas as communication ("We don't talk about Mom's drinking"), the display of emotion ("Men don't cry; it's a sign of weakness"), how boundaries are to be observed ("We don't hug in this family"), the kinds of people who are acceptable ("We don't marry people like that"), and many more. Often it is hard to recognize these rules when we are living in the midst of them. But when we take a step back and look at our family system as a whole, the boundary rules emerge more clearly.

Unwritten Rules

Children who grow up in dysfunctional families quickly learn the unwritten, unspoken rules of the household. Here are some that are especially common:

1. *We don't feel.* We keep our emotions guarded, especially anger (though often there is one person who is allowed to express feelings openly, especially anger).

2. *We are always in control.* We don't show weakness. We don't ask for help, which is a sign of weakness.

3. *We deny what's going on.* We don't believe our senses or perceptions. We lie to ourselves and to others.

4. *We don't trust.* Not ourselves, not others. No one can be relied upon, no one confided in.

5. *We keep the family's secrets.* Even if we told, no one would believe us—or so we think.

6. *We are ashamed.* We are to blame for everything bad that happens—and we deserve it.

Triangles

We are accustomed to thinking of relationships almost entirely in one-to-one terms: my brother and me, my mom and dad, my father and me, and so on. In assessing family systems, we find it is almost always easier to understand how a relationship works by examining it in terms of groups of three, or *triangles*. Instead of speaking about "the relationship I had with my mother," we talk about "the way my mother and I related when we were with my father." This concept is very important and requires more in-depth explanation. We will look at triangles in detail in chapter 5 to see how they help us fill out the patterns revealed by our genogram.

Recurring Patterns

Another important family dynamic revealed by the genogram is the *recurring patterns or generational patterns*. These are personal characteristics or relationship dynamics that get repeated generation after generation within a family. Alcoholism and codependency are common recurring patterns. In part, this is because alcohol appears to have a biological component that is passed along through our genes. But it also reflects attitudinal and behavioral patterns that increase our vulnerability to becoming alcoholic or gravitating to alcoholics as friends and even spouses. Adultery, desertion, abuse and divorce are all patterns of behavior that sometimes seem to be handed down from one generation to the next, and these patterns can be spotted using the genogram.

> *If we do not know about our own family history,*
> *we are more likely to repeat past patterns or*
> *mindlessly rebel against them, without much clarity*
> *about who we really are, how we are similar to*
> *and different from other family members, and*
> *how we might best proceed in our own life.*
> HARRIET LERNER, *THE DANCE OF INTIMACY*[5]

Two of the more general patterns I look for in the genogram are the ones introduced in chapter 3, namely, attachment and adaptability. Do past generations of a family show a tendency to be enmeshed or detached, rigid or chaotic? These are vitally important dynamics that show up very clearly in the genogram.

The Horizontal Axis

The final family dynamic highlighted by the genogram is what is called the *horizontal axis*. Think of it as a sort of timeline on which are noted various key life events that tend to produce stress on the family system. These key events include such things as an untimely death, a divorce, a move or relocation, and other stressful or traumatic occurrences. This dynamic was described as:

> The horizontal flow of anxiety [which] emanates from current stresses in the family as it moves forward through time, coping with the inevitable changes, misfortunes, and transitions in the family life cycle. With enough stress on this horizontal axis, any family will experience dysfunction.[6]

The *horizontal axis* differs from the *vertical axis* in that it relates to current issues within the family that are not cross-generational. As we look at a genogram, we cannot explain everything by the generational patterns. Sometimes problems occur simply because life brings problems.

Horizontal stress is not an excuse for dysfunctional behavior, but understanding the nature and extent of these kinds of stresses can help us understand how dysfunctional behavior arises and is sustained.

Gathering Information

The first step in building your own genogram is to collect information. You will need as much data as possible about your family, going back at least two generations. If you do not have the information to do this, take some time and do the necessary research. Talk to your parents, if they are available and willing to do so. Call your grandparents, your aunts, uncles and cousins. Frequently there will be one family member (for some reason, it is almost always an aunt) who will have been designated as the unofficial family historian and will have already obtained much of the information you will need.

One of our clients, Bill, had a fairly typical experience. When he started asking his parents some basic questions about their families, they became defensive. "Why do you want to know about that?" they asked. "Let the past stay in the past!" Naturally that only stirred up Bill's curiosity.

Over the next several months, he managed to chat with a number of his aunts and uncles. Each was able to give him a few snippets of information, but not enough to fill in the picture completely. He was about to give up when one of his aunts suggested that he talk to one of her cousins. It turned out that this cousin had thoroughly researched her own corner of the family and had enough material about Bill's segment to enable him to complete his genogram.

You may not be as fortunate as Bill was. But even if it takes considerable effort to assemble the data you need, stick with it. It will be worth your trouble.

Building Your Genogram

Once you have assembled the necessary information, it's time to get started. The easiest way to begin is to get several large sheets of paper—perhaps the big sheets that come with demonstration flipcharts. You can purchase these at any office supply store. It is important to use large sheets because genograms tend to take off in all directions as you draw them up, especially when you are just beginning; and because when you are done, you can more easily sit back and study the genogram as a whole.

You will need to know some basic symbols in making your genogram. Let's review them quickly. Male family members are represented by squares, while females are represented by circles. An *X* drawn through a square or circle indicates that the person is deceased. Close relationships between people are indicated by lines: a solid horizontal line between a man and a woman, for example, signifies a marriage. Two slashes through such a line represent a divorce. Children are listed with the oldest on the left and the youngest on the right.

Now let's start building your genogram. Begin with you and your immediate family situation. For example, if you are a married woman with two sons, you would begin like this:

Next, draw the same kind of diagram for your own family of origin. Let's suppose that you are the oldest of three children. You have two younger brothers, and your father has passed away. Adding them to your genogram makes it look like this:

Now do the same thing for your husband's family of origin. For the sake of illustration, let's say he is the younger of two children from his father's second marriage, his father having remarried after the death of his first wife. Let's also say he had a daughter from that first marriage. Sounds pretty complicated, doesn't it? But when you see it diagrammed as part of the genogram, it's actually simple to grasp:

The next step is to add the preceding generation for both sides of the family. I will not even try to describe it in words. Here is what it might look like, though, once you have drawn it up:

You now have a three-generation family tree in place. This is the core of your genogram. That wasn't so hard, was it?

Now go back and add the names of all the individuals and the key dates that relate to them: birth, death, marriage, divorce and any other events from the horizontal axis that seem significant to you. You can see why it is important to use large sheets of paper! When we do a genogram in our counseling rooms, we usually just tape lengths of butcher paper to the wall and start scribbling. The main thing is to just get it all up there somewhere. You can always go back and draw up a tidier version.

Now go back once more and add brief descriptions of any individuals and relationships that were significant, either in your life or in the life of your family. In the case of individuals, you might jot down key character qualities, personality traits, personal problems or notable family roles they played that had a substantial impact on family dynamics. Note especially things like alcoholism or other disorders, those who were the black sheep in their families, and so on.

For relationships, note with a heavier straight line any that were especially close; note with a wavy line any that were particularly strained or conflicted. If you become aware of any "fused pairs" (see page 70), indicate them with a double line. Refer back to the chart on page 85 for a simple guide to these symbols.

A word of caution: Thoroughness is important, but so is clarity. Some people really get into researching their family tree and come up with all kinds of intriguing tidbits of family history, amusing anecdotes, and so forth. Trying to cram too much information onto the genogram will make it impossible to read. Remember, the goal is to identify certain kinds of patterns that repeat from one generation to the next. If you fill in too much extra data, you will not be able to see the forest for the trees! Following the steps outlined here will help you get the most important data into your genogram. If you have additional information you want to keep, you might want to write it up on separate sheets of paper.

Once you have finished constructing your genogram, your task is to sit back, look at the information it presents and reflect on any patterns it reveals. Do any key horizontal axis events appear over and over? What about significant relationship disruptions, such as divorce? Is there a trail of "chaotic" or "enmeshed" families, or of some of the other types of dysfunctional families we mentioned in chapter 3 (generational or family splits, fused pairs, Queen of the Hill families, and so forth)? Do certain types of personal problems repeat themselves (alcoholism or other addictions, emotional breakdowns, and so forth)? One woman, when she looked back through three generations of her family, counted 11 suicides! She had never thought of suicide as a particular problem in her family until it was revealed by her genogram.

To get a better idea of how a genogram works in practice, let's look at a couple of real-life examples. The first is actually a composite of several couples who came to us for counseling over the years.

There was an interesting mixture of love, apathy and tension in the air when Pete and Amy began to tell their story. They had come to us for marriage counseling. Things had actually been deteriorating in their relationship for some time. They were seeking help now that Amy had recently told Pete she couldn't take it anymore and that unless things changed, she was going to file for divorce.

In earlier years, Pete had been a practicing alcoholic. Because of his drinking, he had functioned as an absent member of the family most of the time. When he *was* present, he was hostile and demanding. A few years before, Pete had stopped drinking through sheer willpower. Much of his overt hostility seemed to have dissipated. But the self-centeredness and demanding attitude had remained. By now, Pete and Amy's marriage consisted of little more than two people who happened to live at the same address and who, as a result, occasionally did some things together.

Amy had coped with the barrenness of her marriage by pouring herself into her children, which gave her a sense of purpose. She had also expended tremendous amounts of energy trying to please—or at least to appease—her husband. Her overriding goal was to keep things as calm as possible around the house to avoid provoking any unpleasant reactions from Pete.

Two items precipitated the current crisis in their marriage. First, two of the children had grown up and left home. Amy was faced not only with an empty nest but also with an emptiness in her heart. Second, in an attempt to fill that emptiness, Amy had started to work outside the home. She was doing well at it too; she had already gained several raises and promotions. She was developing new friendships as well. Her success at work only heightened her awareness of how much of life she had missed through the years.

Pete barely noticed that the kids were gone, except for the fact that the house was a bit quieter. But Amy's job bothered him. For a while he tried to blame the problems in their marriage on the fact that she was working. When that failed to find a listening ear, he tried another tack: He made some minor gestures toward greater involvement with Amy and then settled back, thinking that things were improving. But they were not. Pete finally woke up when Amy first used the word "divorce." Before long, they were in our office, seeking help.

I led them through the same exercise I have just described—charting the dynamics of their family system over the past three generations. Their genogram told me a great deal about why they were the way they were. A copy of their genogram is on page 90 so you can refer to it as we go on.

First, look at Pete's side of the family. The dynamics of his parents' relationship were strikingly similar to the dynamics of his own marriage. His father, Ronald, had been an alcoholic who paid little attention to his family most of the time, but he was domineering when he was around. He seemed uncomfortable expressing any kind of emotion. On the other hand, Pete's mother, Sherry, was a nice lady who worked hard to keep the peace in the family—becoming somewhat manipulative and extremely protective of the children in the process. Pete was especially close to his mother but experienced open hostility with his father.

Looking back another generation, we see essentially the same pattern repeated with Pete's grandparents (though apparently without the alcoholism). One trait that shows up clearly and consistently on Pete's side of the family is a strong tendency toward strictness and orderliness, which Pete had continued (and even expanded upon) in his own family.

Now let's look at Amy's side of the genogram. She came from a family in which there was a lot of open hostility between the parents. Her father, Bob, was very domineering, a gambler who was gone a lot but whose presence instilled fear when he was home. On the other hand, he could, at times, function as a "family man" who, despite his other behaviors, managed to convey that his family was important to him.

They often did things together as a family, even though Amy's mother, Pat, was not a healthy person physically. As a result, most of the work for these family events fell on Amy. Amy's mother could display a nasty side, but never toward Amy, for whom she seemed to feel a special closeness.

Amy was unable to learn a great deal about her grandparents. But the little she did find out seemed to indicate, in both cases, a combination of meanness and sweetness, with the men living on the fringes of the family and the women serving as the mainstays of family life.

Pete and Amy's Genogram

Recurring Patterns

The longer we looked at the genogram, the clearer the patterns seemed to emerge. The main thing we saw was a problem with intergenerational boundaries in both families of origin. In each case, the children had become entangled in the parents' problems: Both Pete and Amy found themselves fused with their mothers in an attempt to survive the negative aspects of life with their fathers. As a result, each of them were locked into the patterns they had learned growing up; it was almost impossible for either of them to break away and develop any other style of marriage or family life.

Pete in particular was caught in two very difficult roles at the same time. He was cast in the role of scapegoat by his father, who subtly but unmistakably communicated the notion that "if [he] wouldn't cause so much trouble, this would be a more pleasant place for all of us." At the same time, he was expected to play the role of emotional spouse to his mother when she was feeling alienated from her husband. The two roles reinforced each other in a perverse way. The more Pete's mother leaned on him, the more resentful his father became. Conversely, the more harshly his father treated him, the more Pete's mother tried to protect her "little man." Pete's way of coping with the resulting tension was to withdraw into himself emotionally—and as he grew older, to drown his sorrows in alcohol.

Amy, on the other hand, was clearly taught to assume the role of the "enabler," the one whose steadiness and responsibility make it possible for others to get away with being erratic and irresponsible. She was the one who was expected to stay calm amid the tensions of her parents' marriage. She was the one who would try to comfort both her mother and her father after they fought. She was the one who would try to get the family to act like a family when it seemed that everything was flying apart. It was a tough job for a little girl to fill. But the fear of losing her family and being all alone pushed Amy to almost superhuman effort, balancing all the conflicting emotions in her family. It turned out to be great training for what she experienced with Pete.

Pete and Amy learned some common lessons from their families of origin. Both of them learned, for example, that mother is the source of nurture and that father, as the material provider, is allowed to be emotionally distant most of the time and openly domineering when on the scene. Both also learned very clearly the rule, "We don't talk about our problems."

They also learned some lessons that turned out to be contradictory. For example, Pete learned from his upbringing that a marriage and a family could function with very little shared time. Amy, on the other hand, learned from her family that no matter how bad the problems, you still got together, did things as a family and acted as if everything was just fine.

About 85 percent of us end up marrying someone very similar in personality dynamics to our parent of the opposite sex. . . . We continue what we got used to in childhood.
PAUL MEIER AND FRANK MINIRTH, *FREE TO FORGIVE: DAILY DEVOTIONS FOR ADULT CHILDREN OF ABUSE*[7]

The more clearly we were able to see the dynamics of the families that Pete and Amy grew up in, the more readily we could understand why they had the kind of marriage they had. Pete simply repeated the pattern he had seen modeled by his father, showing little interest in his wife and children. As he drank more and more, the burden on Amy to hold the family together grew heavier.

Pete's retreat from the family triggered in Amy the same fear of abandonment she had experienced growing up. She very naturally slid back into the familiar role of the enabler, taking upon herself full responsibility for holding things together, serving as the children's sole source of nurture. Since neither Pete nor Amy knew how to communicate about what they were feeling and experiencing, the patterns they had learned in childhood were repeated in adulthood. The unresolved hurts of the past were never resolved—just reproduced and intensified.

As I worked with Pete and Amy, helping them understand the dynamics of their respective family systems, two things began to happen. First, the lightbulb began to come on regarding their families of origin. They had already sensed some parallels between themselves and their parents. However, they had not appreciated how their grandparents had shaped their parents' lives. Seeing how dysfunctional patterns could carry over from one generation to the next gave them a better idea of what they were really dealing with.

Second, it became startlingly clear to both Pete and Amy that they were still operating under the same rules and out of the same roles they had known in their families of origin. They were astonished by how precisely they had managed to reproduce the dynamics they had known in childhood in their own marriage and family.

It is not unusual for dissatisfaction to set in with the wife long before the husband senses it, as was the case with Pete and Amy. Men are usually not paying that much attention to relational issues. Much of what we did with them in counseling focused on clarifying, openly and together, the kinds of family rules they *wanted* to establish for their family. They also needed to discuss what roles needed to be abandoned and how they could be replaced by more suitable and flexible roles, both in their relationship with each other and in their relationship with their children.

The Descendants of Abraham

Now let's consider a second example. This one is drawn from the Bible. It concerns Abraham and the generations who followed him.

A few comments as we begin. First, it is obvious that I do not know as much about Abraham and his descendants as I would ordinarily know about people who are still living and coming to me for counseling. I cannot ask Abraham and his family members the many questions that I might like to ask, in order to fill out my understanding of their family system. Thus I must be careful of the dangers that always exist when trying to analyze people who are no longer alive.

At the same time, though, Abraham and his descendants do offer a helpful example of how the genogram works. The Bible actually gives a great deal of information about them (if you want to read more, see the book of Genesis, chapters 12 through 50). And as we will see, the genogram helps illustrate some of the family dynamics that played an important role in biblical history.

To begin with, Abraham and his wife Sarah have been unsuccessfully trying to have children for many years. In desperation, Sarah finally suggests (according to the custom of the times) that Abraham take her maidservant, Hagar, and have a child by her. A son is born, Ishmael. In those days, everything that belonged to a maidservant was considered the property of her mistress. Thus, Ishmael was considered *Sarah's* son.

It's interesting to note that even though Sarah's suggestion that Abraham sleep with Hagar was motivated by her, and it wasn't that unusual in their culture, the result was very similar to what happens in an affair. Sarah and Hagar are at war with each other, so much so that twice Hagar runs away, once before Ishmael was born and once again after he was born. And Abraham withdraws from the conflict, not wanting to add anything to what Sarah is already experiencing.

Some years later, however, Sarah herself gives birth to a son, who is named Isaac. Abraham and Sarah are now, in effect, the parents of two children. Tension soon develops in the family as Sarah begins to reject Ishmael. She says to herself, "Isaac is *mine*—I gave birth to him. But Ishmael isn't *really* mine. He belongs to Hagar." Finally, Sarah's jealousy and resentment build to the point that she prevails upon Abraham to send Hagar and Ishmael away for good.

Here we see the first instance of a pattern that will repeat itself in ensuing generations. The parents play favorites. In this case, they agree together on who the favorite is: Isaac. Ishmael is rejected: first he is rejected emotionally by Sarah, and then literally by both Sarah and Abraham.

Let's look at how the genogram would represent this first generation of Abraham's family:

Isaac and Rebekah

Now let's look at the next generation. Isaac meets Rebekah and falls in love. They marry, and Rebekah gives birth to twin boys, Esau and Jacob. Here is how their genogram would look:

Since Isaac was raised in a family where playing favorites led to such tragic consequences—the banishment of his own half-brother—you would think he would be on guard against this destructive dynamic. In fact, though it takes a somewhat different form in his case, in the end he falls victim to the same problem.

The two sons, Esau and Jacob, develop into very different types of men. Esau is a ruddy outdoorsman; Jacob is more quiet and home-centered. Isaac begins to favor Esau. Rebekah favors Jacob. Did Isaac recognize the unhealthy dynamic that was developing in his family? Did he see it as a repetition of the dynamic he himself had experienced growing up? Did he and Rebekah ever talk about it? We do not know, of course, although there is no evidence to suggest that he did, and much that suggests that "We don't talk about our problems" was a strong unspoken rule in Isaac's family. In any case, the favoritism splits the family right down the middle.

Jacob and Rachel

Now let's build the genogram for Jacob's family. Jacob's marital history is a bit complicated. He sets out to marry his beloved Rachel, but he is duped by his uncle into marrying Leah instead. He angrily confronts his uncle, who tells him to wait a week and allows him to marry Rachel as well. He now has two wives, each of whom has a maidservant, and Jacob has children by all four of them. Here is how the genogram represents Jacob, his wives and his 13 children:

Again the pattern of favoritism continues in Jacob's family. He has two wives competing for his attention, each of whom has some children of her own and some through their maidservants. In this case, since Rachel is the favorite wife, Jacob picks her firstborn son, Joseph, as his favorite son.

The complete genogram for Abraham's family is on page 97. Can you see the patterns that have reproduced themselves from one generation to the next? For example, in each generation, one of the sons has had to leave the family. Abraham's son Ishmael was forced out by Sarah's jealousy. Isaac's son Jacob had to leave out of fear for his life: His brother Esau swore to kill him after Jacob finagled Esau out of his birthright. Jacob's son Joseph was forced to leave because of the jealousy of his brothers, who sold him into slavery.

Each generation also displays a split of some sort between marriage partners that creates an alignment across the generations. Abraham aligns with Isaac against Ishmael. Isaac sides with Esau against Rebekah and Jacob. Jacob aligns himself with Joseph against all his other sons. Can you see how each generation has experienced problems that had their roots in the family dynamics of prior generations? That is a very common occurrence and one that the genogram helps us see very clearly.

Abraham's Genogram

I hope you can now see the value of doing a genogram of your own family. There is an earlier pattern in Abraham's family that ended with Isaac. Twice Abraham lied about Sarah by saying that she was his sister, and each time it led to serious consequences for Pharaoh (see Gen. 12:10-20) and for King Abimelech (see Gen. 20:1-17). Once Isaac does the same thing—lies by saying that Rebekah is his sister. Then King Abimelech sees Isaac caressing Rebekah and confronts him and his lie (see Gen. 26:1-11). Apparently

King Abimelech had been fooled by Abraham, but he wasn't about to be fooled by Isaac. This pattern ends with Isaac—there is no mention that Jacob did anything similar.

There is still one more tool that will add depth to the information on your genogram, and that is being able to look at the three-way relationships in the family.

KEY POINTS TO REMEMBER

1. The genogram gives you understanding about your own actions and behaviors.

2. It also increases your potential for change by showing you who you need to forgive.

3. Boundaries in the family system can either be rigid or diffuse—neither is healthy.

4. Healthy boundaries are always flexible.

5. A genogram helps you see your role in the family, and helps you identify the rules of the family.

6. Your genogram can show you the recurring generational patterns in your family.

Notes

1. H. Norman Wright, *Always Daddy's Girl* (Ventura, CA: Regal Books, 1989), p. 208.
2. Harriet Lerner, *The Dance of Intimacy* (New York: Harper & Row, 1989), p. 199.
3. John and Linda Friel, *Adult Children: The Secrets of Dysfunctional Families* (Deerfield Beach, FL: Health Communications, Inc., 1988), pp. 57-63.
4. Mel Roman, Ph.D. and Patricia Daley, *The Indelible Family* (New York: Rawson Associates, 1980), p. 34.
5. Lerner, *The Dance of Intimacy*, p. 118.
6. Monica McGoldrick and Randy Gerson, *Genograms in Family Assessment* (New York: W. W. Norton & Company, 1985), p. 6.
7. Paul Meier and Frank Minirth, *Free to Forgive: Daily Devotions for Adult Children of Abuse* (Nashville, TN: Thomas Nelson, Inc., 1991), June 21.

Three-way Relationships

We usually think of relationships in terms
of one-to-one interactions. To a family therapist,
however, relationships happen in threes in
what are called triangles. Charting the triangles
in your family can help you understand the
dynamics that made you who you are.

As I mentioned in chapter 4, family systems researchers have found that the best way to study what goes on in a person's relationships is to look at what are called groups of three people, or relational *triangles*.

This is not what most of us would think. If we wanted to understand, for example, the way that a mother and daughter got along, we would probably assume that the logical thing to do would be to focus on just the two of them. What do they do when they are together? How do they relate together? How do they communicate?

For many years researchers operated in just this way, and indeed they did learn a number of helpful things about relationships. But they soon began to find that the inner workings of a relationship were truly unlocked when a third person was added to the picture. When you look at a person within the context of a three-way relationship, you get so much more information about the quality of the relationship and the individuals that make up the triangle.

The Third Person

Let's suppose two people have fallen in love—so deeply that they only have eyes for each other. For months they block out everyone else from their lives. We can study certain aspects of the relationship while they are in this mode. But to a large degree, they are in a world of their own; there is much about their relationship that we will not be able to get a handle on until they are forced to interact with "the outside world."

For example, let's say our two lovebirds have a mutual friend who is dead set against their relationship. When all three of them are together, we are likely to see a very different set of dynamics emerge. We will see how each of them relates to the friend, how they relate to each other in the presence of the friend and—most importantly—how they deal with the challenges their friend is implicitly or explicitly raising in their relationship. All these are very important dynamics, ones we would never have had a chance to observe had we only looked at the original two people.

> *Two-person systems are inherently unstable.*
> *Anxiety and conflict will not stay contained*
> *between two parties for more than a short time.*
> *A third party will quickly be triangled in (or will*
> *triangle himself or herself in). This process*
> *operates automatically, like a law of physics,*
> *without conscious awareness or intent.*
> HARRIET LERNER, *THE DANCE OF INTIMACY*[1]

Looking at these "triangles" thus gives us a new and helpful perspective on relationships. For one thing, the third person provides an outside reference point against which the relationship can be compared. In the case of our two starry-eyed lovers, bringing the skeptical friend into the picture takes them out of the "world of their own" and helps us measure them against the real world.

The third person in a triangle can also serve to uncover hidden dynamics in a relationship. Many husbands and wives, for example, grow accustomed to relating to each other according to established patterns, often with a number of secrets, myths and unspoken rules in operation. When a third person comes along who either does not know the secrets, myths and rules (or who knows of them and simply refuses to go along with them), the couple is suddenly forced to deal with realities they are otherwise adept at ignoring or sidestepping. Triangles help blow the cover of our denial systems.

Perhaps this is connected to the so-called problem of the mother-in-law. What happens to the newlywed couple when one of the mothers comes to visit? Suddenly, uncomfortable questions arise, such as where do one's loyalties lie when mother is in the house? The pressure this puts on the couple brings to the surface much of what is already going on in the marriage.

Charting the Triangles

For these reasons, I have found that examining the triangle relationships in a family is one of the best ways to understand the dynamics of that family system. After completing the family's genogram, the next thing to do is chart the triangles. This chapter will help you understand how three-way relationships work, and how to chart the triangles in your own family system.

This may sound and look very complex and involved. But as you will see, the concepts are not all that difficult to grasp, and the rewards of coming to grips with them are worth it. Our triangles will be drawn using two basic symbols: a straight line drawn between two people, and a wavy line drawn between two people:

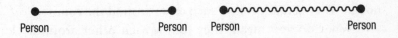

Person   Person   Person   Person

A straight line indicates a relationship of *connection or attraction*. A wavy line indicates a relationship of *aversion or absence of connection*.

Two people who are comfortable together and feel drawn to one another would be linked by a straight line. Two people who do not get along together or who are simply unable to "connect" with each other would be linked by a wavy line.

Another way to think of the lines is to see them as representing either the presence or absence of a rope tying the two people together. The difference between a straight and wavy line is similar to the difference between two people who "can't stay apart" and two people who "can't stay together."

Often, a straight-line relationship will be marked by harmony and attraction, while a wavy-line relationship will be one marked by discord, even by conflict, and especially avoidance. Naturally, we tend to think of a straight-line relationship as one in which the two people get along, and a wavy-line relationship as one in which they don't get along.

But it doesn't always work that way! There are people who remain very strongly attached to each other in a relationship even when that relationship is characterized by a great deal of conflict. Probably all of us know of couples who only seem happy when they are fighting. That may actually be closer to the truth than you think.

The most extreme example of this kind of relationship that I ever came across had to do with the parents of a man named Brock. His parents had been divorced for more than 20 years when I met him, and both had quickly remarried. But according to Brock, over those 20 years, not a day had passed in which they did not get into a fight with each other over the telephone.

"They still talk to each other?" I asked in disbelief. "Every day?"

"Every single day, without exception," Brock said. "And that's not all. They actually follow each other around the country."

"What do you mean, they follow each other around?" I asked.

Brock explained that shortly after their divorce and remarriage, Brock's father and his new wife moved to a different town. Less than a week later, Brock's mother and her new husband moved to the same town. Brock had no idea how or why it happened the way it did. But he said that over the last 20 years, one or the other of his parents had moved more than half a dozen times. Each time it was only a matter of weeks until the other one moved to the same area. The longest they were ever in separate towns was about a month.

As I said, this is an extreme case, but it illustrates the point dramatically. We would have to diagram the relationship between Brock's parents with a straight line. They are clearly connected to each other and seemingly incapable of disconnecting. Yet their relationship has consisted of nothing but conflict for more than 20 years.

By the same token, it is possible for a wavy-line relationship to be relatively peaceful in nature. A wavy line can represent a relationship marked not by conflict but by distance (emotional or geographical), aloofness, coldness, separation, absence (as with a father who is gone 10 months out of the year traveling on business), or simply not being on the same wavelength. A wavy line often indicates the absence of a solid emotional connection, not just the presence of conflict. I have often used a wavy line to describe the relationship between, for example, a parent and a child who never fought or argued at all, simply because they had never managed to forge any kind of meaningful bond.

Usually when we speak of a triangle, we are dealing with a relationship among three flesh-and-blood people who actually interact together on a regular basis. Sometimes, though, the "third person" in a relationship can be more figurative, as when we say things like, "You're just like your mother" or "You remind me so much of your father when you do that." The specter of an absent third party can be a very real presence in a relationship.

Four Types of Triangles

Putting together the various combinations of straight-line and wavy-line relationships produces four types of triangles:

The first triangle is made up of all straight lines. It is one in which all three people are solidly connected with one another and, in most cases, get along with one another comfortably. This is the most pleasant type of triangle relationship for all involved.

The second triangle is made up of all wavy lines. It represents three people who either do not get along at all or who are utterly unable to connect with one another. Obviously, being part of such a triangle would be most unpleasant for everyone.

The third triangle has one straight line and two wavy lines. It reflects what happens when two people align with one another and against the third. Examples of this might be when two brothers pick on a little sister, or when a mother and daughter align against the father.

The fourth triangle consists of two straight lines and one wavy line. This occurs when one person is trying to hold together the others who are at odds—for example, a mother trying to keep the peace between a father and son.

The Principle of Balance

Any of these triangles may exist among any group of three people at any given time. But only two of these types are stable and enduring. As relationships grow in intimacy and intensity, and as they continue over long periods of time, three-way relationships will inevitably gravitate to one or the other of these two types. We call these "balanced" triangles because they will be stable over time.

The first *balanced* triangle is the one composed of three straight lines. It is easy to see why this triangle is able to hold together over time. Everyone involved in it is comfortable with all the others; there is no reason for it to change.

The triangle composed of all wavy lines is *unbalanced* almost by definition. Therefore, it is unstable. How could it be otherwise? A relationship of three people who do not get along is hardly a relationship at all; it is bound to either drift apart or—more likely—self-destruct.

The third triangle, in which two are aligned against one, is also *balanced* and will be stable over time. While it may not represent a very happy arrangement—at least not for the odd man out—it is capable of enduring for a long time. In fact, sometimes the relationship between the two "aligned" parties draws much of its strength from their mutual distaste for the third person. It's like that saying, "The enemy of my enemy is my friend."

The fourth type of triangle, in which one person has a good relationship with two other people who dislike each other, is by nature *unbalanced,* and therefore unstable over time. It may not be immediately obvious why this last triangle is unbalanced. In fact, most of us probably find ourselves in this sort of situation at times. We may, for example, have two co-workers, both of whom we consider our friends, who cannot stand each other. Can such a situation remain unchanged indefinitely?

It can, but only as long as the three of you have fairly structured, impersonal relationships—such as being co-workers in a large office. If the three of you were to move into a small apartment together, things would soon change.

Here's why. Let's say you are the one cast in the role of peacemaker. Sooner or later, one of two things is going to happen. Either you will grow weary from the effort of holding the others together and throw in your lot with one of them against the other, or one of the others will become irritated by your peacemaking efforts and throw in his lot against you! Either way, the relationship becomes two-against-one, which makes for a balanced triangle. (There is, of course, a third possibility: all three of you may get fed up with one another, in which case the relationship breaks down entirely.)

Unbalanced triangles can last in short-term or impersonal situations. But in more intense, long-term settings (and within the family most of all), all triangular relationships will, sooner or later, move to a position of balance.

We actually see this sort of dynamic occur around us all the time. Let's take a simple example. Imagine that you are the parent of a six-year-old girl. One Saturday you invite your daughter's best friend from school to come over to your house for the afternoon. You also invite your child's best friend from church. These two children have never met each other before.

Things go well for a while. But soon the friend from school corners your child and says, "I thought I was your best-best-best friend. Am I?" Your child reassures her that, *of course*, she is her best friend. Immediately this little girl runs to the other guest and says, "I'm her best-best-best friend, and you're not!"

This immediately sends the friend from church running to your child to demand, "Aren't I your best-best-best friend?" And again your child says, "Sure you are." We now have the kind of situation represented by the top unbalanced triangle on page 107.

As any parent knows, before long one of two things is almost certainly going to happen. Either one of the two friends will feel hurt and start whining that she wants to go home, or *both* of the invited guests will become "best friends" with *each other* and ignore your child. We now have the situation represented by the lower balanced triangle.

Children seldom have the maturity and relational skills to resolve this kind of situation in such a way that *everyone* winds up being friends—even with parents' help. When that does happen, we are usually so amazed that we comment about it to others! Nine times out of 10, what happens is that two pair off against one. That is the nature of this kind of triangle, and the reason why we consider it an unbalanced triangle.

The Predictive Power of Triangles

This principle of balance holds true with a remarkable degree of consistency and tenacity. My experience (and that of other family systems theorists) shows that over time, in a close, intimate setting like the family, *all* three-way relationships will inevitably resolve themselves into one of the balanced, and therefore stable, triangle patterns:

Not only that, but the characteristic of any given two-way relationship (whether it is a straight-line or a wavy-line relationship) will remain the same no matter what third party is added.

Sometimes a person will say, "My brother and I always got along great." But then an interesting thing happens. When I draw a triangle to include his mother, there is a straight line between him and his brother. The same thing happens when I draw a triangle to include his sister. But when I try to add in his father, he says, "Well, the three of us never could hit it off together. In that case, you'd have to put a wavy line between my brother and me."

My response would be, "Something's not right here. Experience shows that the quality of your relationship with your brother should remain the same no matter what third party we include." I would then probe more deeply to see if the individual is not either idealizing his relationship with his brother in the first two settings, or wrongly estimating the negative impact of his father in the third setting.

> *Kids aside, we are always in triangles of one sort or another because we always have "stuff" from our first family (as well as elsewhere) that we are not paying attention to and that may overload other relationships. . . . Working on triangles means more than identifying issues with our first family that fuel anxiety elsewhere. It also means observing and modifying our current role in key family triangles.*
> HARRIET LERNER, *THE DANCE OF INTIMACY*[2]

Hidden Dynamics

The consistency of the principle of balance is so reliable that we can often apply it in just this way, to "smoke out" hidden dynamics in relationships. For example, I once dealt with a woman named Betty, whose mother had divorced and remarried when she was young. Betty knew she did not get along well with her mother, who had always been aloof and hypercritical of her. But she believed that her mother and stepfather had a solid relationship. She also insisted that she herself had always felt close to her stepfather as well. When she drew a triangle to represent this relationship, it came out like this.

When I pointed out that the triangle was not balanced, and suggested that Betty take a harder look at the relationships involved, she immediately became defensive—especially about her relationship with her stepfather. "But that's the way it's been!" she insisted. Other members of Betty's group began to ask some probing questions. How had she felt when her mom divorced? How did she really feel when her stepfather first appeared on the scene?

Betty's increasingly agitated responses seemed to indicate there was more going on than met the eye. A picture of Betty's stepfather began to emerge—that of a genial but distant man who provided materially for his family but who seemed to hold his stepdaughter at arm's length emotionally. We began to ask Betty whether she might not be idealizing her relationship with her stepfather. It would have been quite understandable, we assured her, given her estrangement from her mother and the trauma of separation from her father after the divorce to cling to an idealized relationship with her stepfather as a way to guard against feeling like an emotional orphan.

As we continued to talk, Betty suddenly began to weep. "But he was a good man," she sobbed, "a *good* man. Just because he used to . . ."

"Used to *what*, Betty?" we asked gently.

It was then that the painful memories began to rise to the surface. Betty's stepfather had taken advantage of her sexually. Not in extreme ways, and only for a very brief period; but the molestation was nevertheless quite real. The memories were so painful that she had kept them carefully buried for years, all the while telling herself vehemently that her stepfather was "a good man" who loved her. Of course in many ways he was a good man, and he *did* love her. But he had also abused her in a way that had caused her great damage. To face that truth, at a young age, was simply too threatening.

Betty came to see that it was not disloyal to acknowledge the truth about her past; nor would facing up to it destroy her. In fact, bringing it into the open enabled her to deal forthrightly with what had happened, and it proved to be the key to overcoming the depression that had afflicted her for years.

Let's take a look at how charting the triangles works in practice. In chapter 4, we developed a genogram for a couple we called Pete and Amy. As we examine the dynamics of their family and of their respective families of origin, three sets of relationships stand out clearly.

In Pete's family, we saw that his father was an alcoholic who was emotionally distant both from his wife and from his son. At the same time, Pete enjoyed a close relationship with his mother. This three-way relationship, when diagrammed, reflects a classic balanced triangle.

Amy's family of origin displayed a similar pattern. Her father, as we saw, was a domineering man who alienated both his wife and his children. Amy's mother, while not an especially warm person herself, nevertheless seemed to hold Amy in special regard. Again, the relationship among these three forms a balanced triangle.

In both cases, we see exactly the same configuration: a coalition between child and mother, with the father left out. With both Pete and Amy having experienced this pattern growing up, is it any wonder they saw the same pattern develop in their own family? They did not consciously set out to duplicate the pattern they had experienced as children, but all of their life experience tended to be in that direction. Without consciously resisting this dynamic (which they could scarcely be expected to do until they were at least able to recognize its existence), it was simply the most natural pattern for them to fall into. That is precisely what happened.

We could, of course, go much further in our analysis of the triangles in Pete's and Amy's family. They have three children; we could draw a separate triangle representing each of the different three-way relationships represented among the five of them. (For those whose math is a bit rusty, there would be 10 triangles in all.) We would expect to find that each triangle balanced, and that each meshed with the others in terms of whether the various relationships were "straight line" or "wavy line." But this quick glance is enough to demonstrate how useful triangles can be in illustrating family dynamics.

Abraham, Isaac and Jacob

We can also use triangles to better understand some of the dynamics in the families descended from Abraham. Again, we constructed a genogram for Abraham and his descendants in chapter 4. Charting the triangles helps us get a better handle on what happened among some of the key characters.

At the start, when Ishmael was born, all may have seemed well in Abraham's

family. We would represent it with a balanced triangle of all
straight lines. But when we add in Hagar, two of the triangles are
unbalanced. That would explain the tension between Sarah and
Hagar that caused Hagar to leave. But for almost 20 years, this
family lived with that tension.

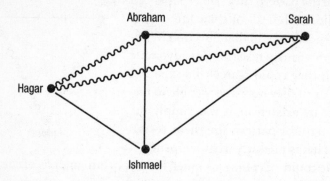

Things got more complicated when Isaac was born. Sarah, as
we have seen, rejected Ishmael and made Isaac her favorite. This
put Abraham in a bind. For him to remain loyal to Ishmael would
have driven Sarah—and, presumably, Isaac—away. Here is how we
would represent the resulting situation.

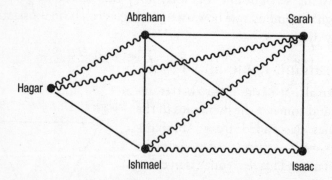

Notice that we overlap Abraham and Sarah's two triangles to
show the interrelationships among the four people. Notice also that
the triangles are in balance. On the other hand, Abraham had another choice. He could align himself with Sarah in rejecting Ishmael.

This, in fact, is what he did. It too resulted in a set of balanced triangles. Everyone is happy because Hagar is now out of the picture.

Now let's look at Isaac's family. In the beginning, Isaac and Rebekah had a beautiful romantic relationship. Then the children came along and things got complicated. Isaac, as we have seen, was drawn to his rugged firstborn son, Esau. Rebekah, on the other hand, favored Jacob. The principle of balance would suggest that we now need to put a wavy line between Isaac and Rebekah. Indeed, when we later read about their interaction after Jacob tricks Esau out of his birthright, we can see the distance and estrangement between them.

Now let's follow the family tree through Jacob's family. Remember that Jacob had planned to marry Rachel, but as a result of his uncle's chicanery he also wound up married to Leah. We can only presume that his relationship with Leah was somewhat strained, and that the relationship between Leah and Rachel was also troubled.

If Jacob plays favorites with his wives, he is also likely to play favorites with his wives' children. He will favor Rachel's son, Joseph, and turn away at least somewhat from the sons borne by Leah and her maidservant and the two sons born by Rachel's maidservant. Again, this is in fact what happens. Here is how we would represent this complex situation using triangles:

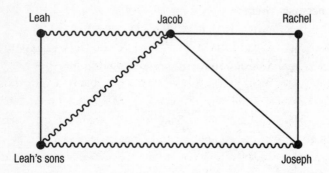

In this case we have three connecting triangles, reflecting the five parties we are considering. Notice that all three triangles are in balance, and the particular one-to-one relationships remain consistent from one triangle to the next.

Again, we are not trying to read more into the stories of Abraham and his sons than is actually in the Bible. But we are told a great deal about this sprawling clan. Charting the triangles helps us see and understand some of the dynamics at work. In this case, we see a pattern of parental favoritism repeating itself in one generation after the other. The different ways each generation resolves the tensions that it creates have repercussions down through the years.

Charting *Your* Triangles

No doubt you can see that charting the triangles for a family can become a fairly complicated process. To some degree, this is simply a matter of numbers. The more people involved, the more triangles there will be. I once worked with a family that had 15 children. If we had worked out every conceivable three-way combination, we would have had to draw 455 triangles! You can see why the arrival of each additional child makes family life so much more complex!

Charting the triangles is also tricky because, as we have seen, the dynamics of relationships are not always clear and simple, and not always what they seem to be at first glance. It can be difficult to completely work out the triangles for your family without the hands-on assistance of an experienced counselor.

Even so, you can learn a lot about your family by charting the triangles to the extent that you *are* able to do so. Go back to the genogram you built in chapter 4. Starting with a fresh sheet of paper, first draw triangles to represent any three-way relationships that you feel confident you understand. Do this both for your own family and for previous generations, as you are able. Then see if you can draw other triangles based on the information from those you have just drawn.

What do the triangles tell you? Do they help you understand where potential conflict points in your family may have been? Are you able to detect patterns from one generation to the next, like the ones we saw in our examples? Most important of all, do they help you see more clearly how the dynamics of your family life affected *you*? Do they point out particular relationships that did not work well, particular individuals whose impact on you was harmful in some way?

If so, your tendency may be to get angry or bitter at such individuals. That would be an understandable reaction. But our goal has not been simply to nail down who did what to whom so that blame and bitterness can be more accurately targeted. Rather, our goal has been to get a clearer picture of where the damage lies *so that you can respond to it constructively.*

Now What?

Up to now, I have focused our energies on understanding how families work—in particular, how they sometimes "go wrong." We have seen how important our family system is in making us who we are. We have seen what a "normal," or healthy, family looks like, and we have reviewed some of the most common ways in which families fall short of this and become dysfunctional. We have also looked at some of the roles, rules, myths and secrets that may have been present in your own family.

If you drew up a genogram of your family and worked out the triangles for as many of the relationships as you could, you should now have a clearer idea of what went right and what went wrong in your particular family. You may well have spotted various dynamics that have affected you negatively, and whose impact is still with you to this day.

In most cases, examining our families in this way points us to certain people in our past who seem like "villains." Their weaknesses, their limitations, their failure to do things they should have done, their having done things they should *not* have done—all may have contributed to difficulties that are still with us in our lives today. The "villain" may be a parent or other adult figure. It may be a brother or sister. Some people even wind up angry at God, for *allowing* bad things to happen to them.

But the important thing is not just discovering where the problems and who the villains are. The important thing is what we *do* with this information now that we have it. Whatever may have been done to us while we were children, we are now grown-ups who must *take responsibility* for our attitudes and actions. Whatever others may have done in the past, what matters is what *we* do *today*.

It is not enough for us to label others as villains and blame them for all our troubles. We need to understand what has been done to us so that we can take responsibility for our lives as adults and find freedom from our past hurts. We cannot change what has happened to us. But we can learn to respond to what has happened to us in a way that helps us rise above the negative influences of the past.

How can you learn to respond in such a way that you can begin to experience the freedom of forgiveness? What about those who have hurt you? Can they be released from their pain as well? In Part Two you will discover that there can be release for you and for others if you and they learn the lesson of forgiveness.

KEY POINTS TO REMEMBER

1. To understand relationships, you need to look at them in the context of three people in the system.

2. Three-way relationships are described as the triangles on the genogram.

3. There are four possible ways that three people can relate.

4. There are two ways a triangle can be stable over time.

5. There are two ways that three people interact that are full of tension and instability.

6. Understanding your relationship triangles can predict potential problems and patterns.

7. Relationship triangles help to expose hidden dynamics in a family system.

8. The triangles in your genogram help you know where the work of forgiveness begins.

Notes
1. Harriet Lerner, *The Dance of Intimacy* (New York: Harper & Row, 1989), p. 151.
2. Ibid., p. 160.

PART TWO

The Freedom of Forgiveness

Forgiving Others, Releasing Ourselves

Once you realize how deeply those in your family
may have hurt you, forgiving them may seem like the
last thing you want to do. But, in fact, forgiveness is
crucial to your spiritual and emotional health. It is
the key to freedom from the pain of the past.

When Marti, whom we met in chapter 3, first came for help, she had no intention of dragging her mother into the picture. She was struggling with insecurity and fearfulness, which she did not relate to problems within her family. But as we talked (and especially as we constructed her genogram and mapped out the triangles representing her family relationships), the connection became increasingly clear, especially with regard to her mother. Marti was in her forties, but she was still a little girl in terms of her relationship to her mother.

The more we probed this area, the more Marti became aware of how her mother had damaged her, and the more the anger she had bottled up inside came to the surface. One day she turned to me and demanded, "Where is all this going to take me, this therapy? Where is it going to lead?"

I studied her calmly for a moment before replying. "Do you really want to know?" I asked finally.

"Yes!" she snapped. "Yes, I really want to know!"

"Well, Marti," I said, "ultimately, if all goes well, you'll come to the point where you can forgive your mother for the harm she has done you."

"Forgive her?" Marti cried. "*Forgive* her? I will *never* forgive her! Never!"

Marti's reaction wasn't all that unusual. People often recoil at the notion of forgiveness. It is not hard to see why. The early phase of counseling often proceeds along the lines of Part One of this book, with an in-depth exploration of the ways our family dynamics have worked against us. Once people have a clear picture of the harm that others have caused them, it's easy to see why forgiving those people might not be the first thing that comes to their mind. "What do you mean?" they cry. "After all that person did to me? After all the pain and confusion he (she) caused me? You expect me to *forgive* him, just like that?"

My answer is always, "I understand why you are reacting the way you are. I know that in your hurt and anger, forgiving the ones who have damaged you may be the last thing you feel like doing. In fact, I *don't* expect you to forgive them 'just like that.' Forgiving others is not an easy thing. It takes time and effort. But I think you will come to see that ultimately you *must* forgive if you are to be truly free. Forgiveness releases you, not the other person."

Forgiveness breaks the cycle. It does not settle all questions of blame and justice and fairness; to the contrary, often it evades those questions. But it does allow relationships to start over. In that way, said Solzhenitsyn, we differ from all animals. It is not our capacity to think that makes us different, but our capacity to repent, and to forgive. Only humans can perform that most unnatural act, and by doing so only they can develop relationships that transcend the relentless law of nature.
PHILIP YANCEY, "AN UNNATURAL ACT"[1]

Like Marti, you may have been hurt deeply by some important people in your life. As a result of working through the exercises found in Part One, you may be more aware than ever of just how much you have been hurt. And your feelings toward them may be anything but merciful and forgiving. Nevertheless, I am going to urge you on to the high and hard duty of forgiveness, because long experience has shown me that it is the only way to attain genuine freedom from the bad effects of the past. It is the only way to put to rest the issues of your past.

Why Forgive?

We *must* learn to forgive those who have hurt us: that is the message of this book. Forgiveness is important for at least two reasons. We will discuss them in more detail as we go along. For now, let's just note what they are.

First, and very important for our present discussion, forgiveness is important for our own sake. I sometimes shock people by telling them they need to learn to be "selfish" about their forgiveness. Often they stare back at me in disbelief. "What do you mean?" they ask. "You want me to be *selfish*? But selfishness is wrong, isn't it?"

Indeed it is. And I do not mean to be taken absolutely literally, as if we should live our lives in an utterly "me-first" mode. But there is an appropriate way of caring for ourselves that can factor into forgiveness.

It is similar to what happens when you get on an airliner and the flight attendant explains how to use the oxygen mask that drops into your lap if the plane loses cabin pressure. She tells you that if you are traveling with a child or someone else who requires assistance, you should put your own mask in place first, and *then* help the other person. In the same way, if we are going to take a loving concern for others—and we certainly should—we must also take a loving concern for ourselves. Selfishness says, "Me first; who cares about you?" Appropriate self-care says, "I'm going to take care of me *so that* I can take care of you."

Second, forgiveness is important for God's sake. Every wrong is an offense first and foremost against a wise and loving God who does not wish to see any of His creatures harmed and who takes it personally when they are wronged. As we will see, an important part of our being able to work out our own forgiveness is drawn from the forgiveness that God Himself has shown us.

Canceling the Debt

Just exactly what does it mean to forgive someone? Does it mean to ignore what he or she has done? To pretend that it never happened—to forget it? To cover things up on the outside while the anger and hurt continue to boil on the inside?

No. Forgiveness is both simpler and more complex than that. The best way I know to understand forgiveness actually comes from the world of banking. Let's say you go to the bank and take out a loan. You now owe money to the bank, which you have every intention of repaying. But let's also say that something unforeseen comes up: a financial calamity or a major health problem, something that makes it impossible for you to keep up with your loan payments.

What does the banker do? He could simply insist that you pay back the loan anyway. "I don't care about your problems," he might say. "Just pay me what you owe me." He could keep that debt hanging over your head for the rest of your life.

Or he could, if he was concerned about his bottom line and had done everything possible to collect the debt, decide to release you from your obligation. "I'm canceling the debt," he might say. "You don't owe me anything. From here on, I consider us 'even.'" In banking terminology, that is called *forgiving* the loan. It is exactly what we are called to do in our dealings with those who harm us. Of course, when a bank does that, there are consequences in terms of banking—it will be a long time before we can get another loan. But the original loan is canceled—forgiven.

That's the same concept as in the biblical understanding of forgiveness. In Colossians 2:13, Paul writes, "You were dead because of your sins and because your sinful nature was not yet cut away. Then God made you alive with Christ, for he forgave all our sins." Now, if I were able to interact with Paul, I might ask, "How did God do that?" And Paul answers in the next verse: "He canceled the record of the charges against us and took it away by nailing it to the cross" (v. 14).

When Paul says, "He canceled the record of the charges against us," he is describing our debt. Here it is not money; it is the debt of our sin. And like the servant in Matthew 18, it is a debt we cannot pay. So for Paul—and for God—the debt is canceled. And so that we know it is really canceled, Paul says that it has been "nailed to the cross." That's the biblical understanding of forgiveness. In fact, the primary Greek word used for forgiveness in the New Testament means "to cancel a debt."

When someone does us wrong, when he or she causes us pain, we often feel as though that person has taken away something that belonged to us—our peace, our joy, our happiness, our dignity—and that he now *owes* us something. We are like a miserly banker, holding an IOU against someone who can never hope to repay us. "I don't care about your problems," we say. "You've hurt me, and you're going to pay." But when we forgive the person, we simply release him from his debt. We do not have to pretend the debt never existed. We just forgive it: "You no longer owe me anything."

Who Benefits?

Forgiveness has three beneficiaries, or aspects. First, it has to do with the other person. That is obvious. But second, it also has to do with God, who is—to stretch our analogy a bit—the ultimate creditor, the one to whom all our "debts" are ultimately due. And finally, it has to do with *us*. When we release others from their debts, we also release ourselves from the painful effects of what they did to us. It is a paradox, but it is absolutely true; when we harbor bitterness against others, that bitterness eats away at *us*. The only way to get the poison out of our system is by forgiving.

I said a moment ago that forgiveness has to do with God. Actually, forgiveness is intimately bound up with the very essence of God. He Himself is forgiving by nature and wants us to be forgiving too. There are places in the Bible in which we are urged to show forgiveness to others:

"Forgive us our sins, as we have forgiven those who sin
against us" (Matt. 6:12).

"Be kind to each other, tenderhearted, forgiving one another, just as God through Christ has forgiven you"
(Eph. 4:32).

"Make allowance for each other's faults, and forgive anyone who offends you. Remember the Lord forgave you, so
you must forgive others" (Col. 3:13).

What stands out in these passages is that forgiveness begins
with God. He does not say, "Forgive or else." He says, "Forgive others *as I have forgiven you.*" The reason we can show mercy to others
is because He has shown mercy to us. In fact, you could almost say
that the mercy we show to others *is* the mercy He shows to us. We
simply receive it and pass it on. In other words, our *forgiveness* flows
from our *forgiveness.*

In answer to a question from one of His disciples, Jesus told
this story. Peter had asked, "How many times must I forgive those
who hurt me?" In other words, "Just how far does this forgiveness
business go? Surely there's a limit to it, right? I mean, if someone
just keeps on hurting me, I don't have to keep on forgiving him, do
I? Surely there comes a point when I say, 'That's enough!'"

Jesus' answer makes it clear, however, that there *is* no limit to
forgiveness. The number of times someone has hurt us is not the
issue. Whether the other person deserves forgiveness is not the issue. *How we respond to God's grace* is the issue. We show mercy to
others because He has shown mercy to us.

Someone has said that forgiveness is a "unilateral process." This
means it is something we do on our own, regardless of whether
the other person responds. So many times we say, "I'll forgive him
if he . . ." or "I'll never forgive her *until she* . . ."

But there are no "ifs" or "untils" in forgiveness. It is something
we do all by ourselves, whether or not the one we are forgiving even
knows or cares we are doing it.

This is important to understand because it sets us free to forgive. We can obtain the wonderful release that comes with forgiving others even without their cooperation!

Forgiveness involves letting go. Remember playing tug-of-war as a child? As long as the parties on each end of the rope are tugging, you have a "war." But when someone lets go, the war is over. When you forgive your father, you are letting go of your end of the rope. No matter how hard he may tug on the other end, if you have released your end, the war is over for you.
H. NORMAN WRIGHT, *ALWAYS DADDY'S GIRL*[2]

Recognizing Our Need

Jesus makes another point about forgiveness while He is having dinner at the home of a prominent religious leader, a Pharisee named Simon. They are sitting and talking together when a woman from the town makes an unscheduled appearance. Read what happens next. "When a certain immoral woman from that city heard he was eating here, she brought a beautiful alabaster jar filled with expensive perfume. Then she knelt behind him at his feet, weeping. Her tears fell on his feet, and she wiped them off with her hair. Then she kept kissing his feet and putting perfume on them" (Luke 7:37-38).

Needless to say, Simon is shocked. Jesus becomes aware of Simon's indignation and tells the story of two men who were in debt to a moneylender. (It is worth noting, by the way, that in those days a moneylender was *not* the equivalent of our modern savings and loan officers. He was more like what we would call a loan shark. Falling behind in your payments could be a risky business.) One of the men owed 50 silver coins; the other owed 500. Astonishingly, the moneylender decided to forgive both debts. Jesus asks Simon, "Who do you supposed loved him more after that?" Simon says, "I suppose the one for whom he canceled the larger debt" (vv. 42-43).

Jesus congratulates Simon for giving the correct answer. Then He points out that Simon had failed to perform some of the customs that were considered to be part of a good host's duty in those days. "Look at this woman kneeling here. When I entered your home, you didn't offer me water to wash the dust from my feet, but she has washed them with her tears and wiped them with her hair. You didn't greet me with a kiss, but from the time I first came in, she has not stopped kissing my feet. You neglected the courtesy of olive oil to anoint my head, but she has anointed by feet with rare perfume" (Luke 7:44-47).

Do you sense the sting in these words? Jesus is saying to Simon, "I know this woman has done unspeakable things. But she knows it too, and she recognizes the marvel of God's mercy toward her. That's why she is showing such love and devotion. On the other hand, Simon, you barely showed me the most basic hospitality when I came to your home as a guest. Perhaps that is because you haven't yet realized how merciful God has been to you. Or do you suppose that you have no need of God's mercy? That you are not, in your own way, as needy as this poor woman?"

The point is that we are *all* people in need of God's mercy—indeed, we are all people who have *received* God's mercy. The key is for us to recognize it and to let it shape the way we treat others. We must let our *forgiven-ness* express itself in *forgiveness*.

The Process of Forgiveness

The process of forgiveness always begins first with a decision. It is an act of the will, something we choose to do because we know it is healthy and right, even though we may not feel like it at the moment. I *choose* to take the path that leads to forgiveness. I *decide* to work toward releasing you from the debt you owe me.

Second, forgiveness then becomes a process that involves freeing *ourselves* from the emotional effects of what was done to us. When someone has hurt us deeply, it is one thing to say to the person, "I forgive you." We can say it with great earnestness, and even *mean* it sincerely. But the pain, the resentment, the confusion caused by the person's wrong action is still there. Sometimes we have to work through our feelings before we can finish the process of canceling the debt. Often we find that even *after* we have made the decision to forgive, our emotions rise up again and make us want to re-impose the debt.

For example, let us say that you have done something that hurts me. To take a simple example, let's say that while visiting my house, you break a vase that has been in my family for years. You apologize and ask forgiveness. Now what do I do? First, even though I am still feeling sad about the loss of my vase—and still feeling angry at you for breaking it—I know that the right thing to do is to forgive you. And so I do.

At this point, in one sense, the debt has been canceled. I have forgiven you, and that is that. But in another sense, I probably still have some work to do. I may look at the spot on the shelf where the vase used to be and feel upset that my family heirloom has been destroyed. I may find that I am still irritated at you for destroying it. In time, I realize I am once again holding against you the "debt" you incurred when you broke my vase, even though I forgave you.

Now what do I do? I go back to my decision—I have released you from the debt you owe me—I have forgiven you. But now I have to work through all of my feelings about what has happened. I give validity to my loss. I accept the reality of my feelings. I am hurt by your carelessness. I am angry at the loss of something that was important to me. I am saddened over the fact that the vase is gone. I need to "work through" these feelings a number of times before I can finally let go of my anger and feel like I have completely forgiven you.

This is what we call the *process* of forgiveness, the process by which I not only release *you* emotionally, but I also find release for *myself*. In time it can happen that virtually *all* the bitterness and hurt are released. I still have a mental recollection of what happened (I am aware that you carelessly broke my vase), and I am still aware of negative consequences that resulted from what you did (my vase can never be replaced). But what happened between us is no longer a "live issue" in the way I think of you and relate to you, or in the way I live my life. This is the third part of the forgiving process—I have closed the book. The debt is fully canceled. I have completed the process of forgiveness. (We will have more to say later about the matter of forgiving and forgetting.)

The Six Steps of Forgiveness

Let's look at how the threefold process of forgiveness works in practical terms. Once we have made the decision to forgive, there are six main steps we will experience. We will briefly review them here. In later chapters we will look more closely at some of the questions and issues that arise as we actually set about the process of working through them.

1. Recognize the Injury

"All right," Gail sighed. "I'm ready. I can finally admit my anger over what my parents did to me. I'm tired of getting my head messed up going back and forth between making excuses for them and denying that anything ever happened in the first place. My dad molested me and I feel incredible rage toward him. I feel just as much rage toward my mother because she let it continue all those years. There. That's what happened, and that's how I feel about it."

After more than a year of therapy, being part of a support group for adults who had been molested as children, Gail was engaged in the process of releasing her parents, and herself, from the grip of what had happened in the past.

The process of forgiveness begins when we feel some kind of pain, hurt or injury. We need to answer some questions: What happened? Who did it? What effect did it have on me? We need to work hard at coming to grips with what happened. Often we are aware of pain and hurt, but we have buried the *cause* of those feelings deeply. We have a hard time remembering what actually happened because part of us does not really want to remember what happened. But the remembering is important.

Back in chapter 1, we met Larry, whose parents had literally abandoned him when he was five years old. Even though it quickly became clear that both his parents had been severe alcoholics and had mistreated him in many ways, Larry had somehow managed to place the blame on himself for everything that had happened. He was at the end of his rope, emotionally and in every other way.

Then one day in the clinic, he and his therapy group were hearing a presentation on the difference between "wrongs done *by* us" and "wrongs done *to* us." Larry suddenly jumped up from his chair. For the first time, he realized that he had been injured, that he had been sinned *against.* That realization triggered a host of memories. For the first time, he was able to remember things that had happened to him in childhood, and to understand them properly. He finally recognized the injuries that had been done to him as a child.

Larry said later, "I suddenly realized that I had spent a lifetime turning all my hurt, angry feelings into confessions of things I had done wrong. I even confessed to things I *knew* I hadn't done, just in case." Remembering the past was the crucial first step in Larry's coming to grips with his past.

This, then, is where the process begins. You might want to get a sheet of paper and make a list of the "wrongs done to me." Be accurate and objective. The goal is not to wallow in self-pity but to lay a foundation of understanding for the steps that are to follow. Take the time necessary to make the list as complete as possible. Reviewing your genogram will help you identify likely patterns of "wrongs done to me" that are characteristic of your particular family.

2. Identify the Emotions Involved

As you become aware of the injuries you have experienced in your life, you must also try to identify the feelings associated with those injuries. For most of us, three types of emotions will predominate.

Fear. The emotions we associate with past injuries will generally be a composite of what we felt when the injury first occurred and what we are feeling now. The feelings from childhood when many of the injuries will have taken place will usually be dominated by fear. It is not hard to see why. Usually, the ones who hurt us as children were grown-ups; people we often looked up to and respected. It was natural for us to be afraid of them, and often we carried over that fear into our present-day experience.

Guilt and shame. Adult children of dysfunctional families sometimes seem to have a corner on the guilt market. Most of it is false guilt. We find ways to blame ourselves for our problems, even for things we did not do, just as Larry did. Clarifying exactly what happened helps clear away this kind of false guilt.

It also helps in dealing with shame. Guilt and shame are not the same thing. To put it simply, guilt has to do with *what we have done,* and shame has to do with *who we are.* When we do something wrong and feel badly about it, that is guilt. When we conclude that we are a terrible person because of what we have done, that is shame.

We need to be careful not to let sinful actions lead to shameful self-definitions. If I lose my temper, it is not helpful for me to say, "I'm just an angry person who can never keep his big mouth shut."

Shame makes us want to hide from others lest they find out "what we're really like." We become convinced that there is something inherently wrong with us. Shame almost always accompanies guilt. It is important to recognize both feelings and to deal with each one appropriately.

Anger. When we begin to come to grips with the harmful things that have been done to us, and with the feelings of fear, guilt and shame that those injuries have produced, it usually isn't too long until anger surges to the surface. Many people are astonished at the amount of anger—"rage" is not too strong a word—they have been carrying around with them, stuffed deep inside, for years and years.

Anger is not necessarily a bad thing. There *is* such a thing as righteous anger. It is often an entirely appropriate reaction to having been damaged. In counseling, I find that it is important for people to be able to identify their anger. It clears their vision and helps them see the truth. It also makes it easier for them to continue with the process of forgiveness.

3. Grieve What Was Lost by Expressing Your Hurt and Anger

I treat this as a separate step because it is so important. It is not enough to simply identify what we are feeling. We also need some way to *express* our feelings, especially our anger.

If you discovered that there was poison in your belly, it would not be enough just to know it was there, or even to know exactly what kind of poison it was. You would want to get rid of it! That is what the word "express" actually means. It means to "press something out," like squeezing the juice from a lemon. "Expressing" our destructive emotions is important because it gets them "out of our system" so that they cannot poison us any longer.

There are several concrete things we can do to express our feelings. One is simply to talk them out with a trusted friend. Make sure to find someone who is willing to listen without trying to problem-solve.

Another way to express feelings is to write them out. Take a sheet of paper and begin writing: "Today I feel about this situation . . ." and then complete the sentence in as much detail as you can. Don't stop to rework or rewrite as you go. The goal is not to produce a piece of enduring literature but to get your feelings out. Once you have finished writing, you may want to share what you have written with a friend. Some people find it easier to interact with others about sensitive topics if they can "work from a script" in this way.

A variation on this technique is to write a letter to the person who hurt you, stating what happened and how it made you feel. One man I know wrote a letter to his long-deceased father, pouring out the disappointment and hurt he felt when his father died. As he wrote, he became aware that he was actually feeling anger at his father for abandoning him just when he needed him most. Writing the letter helped him organize his thoughts and clarify his emotions. Some people write a series of such letters, one for each person who harmed them in the past.

It is extremely important that you *never* send these letters to the people to whom they are addressed. That is not the intention of writing these letters. You gain nothing by "getting even." Your purpose in writing these letters is to help clarify your feelings and emotions. Sometimes you may feel the need to send something to the person involved. If you do, it should be a much-revised version that has lain on your desk unmailed for some weeks as you work through your expectations in sending the letter.

If you don't like to write, you can talk to an empty chair in which you imagine the other person is sitting. Tell the person what you remember and what you are feeling. Some people find it helpful to switch sides—to figuratively (or even literally) sit in the other chair and try to comprehend the other person's likely reactions and responses.

Talking to an empty chair may feel a bit ridiculous, rather like talking to yourself. But actually, talking to ourselves is a very important aspect of expressing our feelings. The fact is, we all talk to ourselves constantly—we maintain a constant running monologue inside our heads. Making our self-talk explicit helps us understand what is going on inside.

When we hear something often enough, over a long enough period of time, we tend to believe it. This kind of repetition can work against us, as when we constantly tell ourselves, "What a jerk I am." But it can also work *for* us. Healthy self-talk can help us change and grow. The rule for healthy self-talk is simple: Make positive statements, in the present tense, that reinforce the values, attitudes and self-concepts you are trying to develop. Don't say what you will do in the future; just reaffirm what is already true. "I am a worthwhile person because God loves and accepts me. I am working on forgiving my parents and getting free of the hurts of my past."

4. Set Boundaries to Protect Yourself

Boundaries are limits. They are like a fence that we put around our house to define where our property begins and ends, and to keep it separate from other people's property. As children, our personal boundaries were often violated. Physical and sexual abuse are obvious violations. Other ways that parents might have ignored their children's personal boundaries include: opening the door and coming into the bathroom when the child is in there; a father walking in on a teenage daughter while she is dressing; a parent going through a child's drawers or papers without the child's permission, or even reading a child's locked diary.

Some parents see this as their "right." But each is a violation of an important boundary. If this happened to you as a child, it has made it difficult for you as an adult to set appropriate boundaries in your relationships. You may even have to be convinced that you have the right to set boundaries for yourself.

In our earlier discussion on types of dysfunctional families, we learned about the Attachment Scale. We saw that some families are "Disengaged," meaning that the members live as isolated islands with almost no involvement in one another's lives. Others are "Enmeshed," meaning they are so tangled up in one another that it becomes impossible to tell where each member's identity ends and begins. In working through the process of forgiveness, it often becomes necessary for a person to establish some new boundaries, to give himself or herself space to work in.

Often these boundaries have to do with the way we relate to others, or the way we let them relate to us. For example, we might decide, "From now on, I will decline to accept my mother's suggestions on what I should wear, or how I will do my hair, or how I will clean my house." Or, "I will listen to the advice my dad gives me about how I'm raising my kids, but I won't let myself feel that I have to do anything he says."

In many cases, setting boundaries means that we need to physically stay away from other family members, either for a time or for good. I remember Penny, age 22, who had been in and out of several mental health facilities by the time she came to us for help. Each time she went into the hospital, she would make remarkable progress. But within a few months of her release, she would need to go back.

When we constructed her genogram and charted the triangle relationships in her family system, it became obvious that Penny occupied the role of scapegoat in her family. When she was away from them, she did well. But as soon as she returned to her family, she relapsed into her old problems.

Penny decided she needed to live apart from her family for a time. She rented an apartment of her own. When she was released from the hospital, she went there instead of going home. She explained to her family what she was doing and promised to write them a postcard each week to let them know how she was doing. Her family did not like the arrangement and tried to sabotage it, but Penny stuck to her guns.

It was three months before Penny felt that she was able to begin relating to her family again. She began making periodic phone calls, being careful to limit their frequency and duration, and reviewing the kinds of topics she would and would not talk about with her parents. Once when Penny tried to enforce a boundary she had set, by telling her father she did not want to talk about a certain topic with him, he got angry and hung up on her.

Penny was in anguish. Had she done the right thing? She wrestled with the temptation to call her father back and apologize to him. But then she thought everything through carefully and decided that she had been right to do what she did. The next day, her father called *her* back. She was elated. "For the first time," she said, "he treated me like I was a real person. It's as though he's started to accept the fact that I'm an adult, and that I have boundaries."

Most people find that some boundaries are only temporary. They give a little extra space while they work through particular difficulties. Other boundaries, however, become permanent. They help make a lasting change for the better in the dynamics of our family system.

5. Cancel the Debt

Now it is time to forgive—to cancel the debt. This is the third piece of the three-part process of forgiving. First, make the decision to forgive. Second, process the emotions related to forgiving and set appropriate boundaries if necessary. Third, make the decision to finalize the forgiving.

As we have worked through our injuries and emotions, we may have felt a sense of someone owing us something. That is a useful experience, because it helps us identify where we are holding emotional IOUs and where we need to forgive.

Often it helps to make the act of forgiveness take some concrete, tangible form. For example, some people take the letters they have written to various family members and write "canceled" across them. I know others who have burned or even buried their lists of injuries to show that all those wrongs are now dead and buried.

Again, it may seem awkward to engage in these kinds of exercises. But my experience is that it can be helpful. Such actions leave a person with the memory of a definite time when he or she tangibly and concretely canceled his or her debts. The person need never be troubled by the nagging thought, *Perhaps I really didn't forgive them,* or *Maybe it wasn't really complete.* He or she knows it happened—it was real. If this describes what you are ready to do, it can also help to talk about your act of forgiveness with someone who will understand.

6. Consider the Possibility of Reconciliation

Earlier, I said that forgiveness is unilateral; it is something you can do all by yourself, without the other person cooperating with it or even being aware of it. Reconciliation is different. If two people who have been estranged from one another are going to be reconciled, both must be involved. I can desire to be reconciled with you; but if you refuse to be reconciled with me, there is nothing I can do but wait and hope that your heart will change.

We will look at reconciliation in more detail later. For now, let's simply note that reconciliation is the ideal outcome of the process of forgiveness—when it is possible. But it is not always possible. Remember, six steps will help you through the process of forgiveness:

The Six Steps of Forgiveness

1. Recognize the injury.
2. Identify the emotions involved.
3. Grieve what was lost by expressing your hurt and anger.
4. Set boundaries to protect yourself.
5. Cancel the debt.
6. Consider the possibility of reconciliation.

Forgiveness is a process that leads you to forgive all those who have hurt you (including, as we will see, yourself!). It also leads you to seek and accept forgiveness from those *you* have harmed. If your forgiveness is genuine, you will be willing to see it move in both directions: from others toward you, from you toward others. Forgiveness is the key to freedom from the effects of your past.

KEY POINTS TO REMEMBER

1. Forgiveness is important for your own sake—you are the one who benefits the most.

2. Forgiveness is important for God's sake—He has shown us how to forgive.

3. The definition of forgiveness is "to cancel a debt."

4. True forgiving comes out of your being forgiven.

5. You must know what you are forgiving—there are no blanket acts of forgiveness.

6. Forgiving involves grieving over what has been lost.

7. Forgiving occurs in the context of healthy boundaries.

8. You can forgive and not be reconciled, but you can't be reconciled without forgiving.

Notes
   1. Philip Yancey, "An Unnatural Act," *Christianity Today* (April 5, 1991), p. 37.
   2. H. Norman Wright, *Always Daddy's Girl* (Ventura, CA: Regal, 1989), pp. 235-236.

Forgiving and Forgetting

We all know the old adage, "Forgive and forget."
But forgetting the harmful things that have happened
to you is precisely the wrong thing to do. You must
work hard at remembering—and accepting—what
has happened in order that you may truly forgive.

Myra burst into tears. I have seldom heard anyone sob so deeply. I was at a loss to understand this sudden outburst; I had no idea what had caused it. So I sat quietly and waited.

"I can't, that's all," she said. "I just can't."

"You can't what?" I asked gently.

Silence. By now in our discussions, I had learned that Myra's father had physically and sexually abused her from the time she was 11 years old until she ran away from home at 17. Later, Myra had married a fine man named Greg, a widower with one son; they now had a daughter of their own. Their marriage was good. They appeared to be a happy family.

Myra had come to me for counseling because she wanted to get free of the bitterness and resentment she felt toward her father. We had met together a few times, and she seemed to be coming to grips with her misery-filled childhood. But today, before we had even gotten started, the tears had begun to flow.

"Myra, *what* can't you do?" I asked again. She slowly lifted her head and looked at me through tear-filled eyes. "I can't forget what he did to me," she sobbed. "I've tried. I've really *tried*. But I just can't!" She buried her head in her hands and wept quietly.

I waited a moment, and then said simply, "But, Myra, you don't have to forget."

She looked up at me again, a bewildered look on her face. "Say that again," she said.

"You don't have to forget what your father did to you," I repeated.

"But . . . then how can I . . . I mean . . ." Myra stammered.

"Myra, who told you that you had to forget what happened?"

She pulled back in her chair, really confused now. "Why—why, the Bible says so. Doesn't it?"

"I've never read that in the Bible anyplace," I said.

"But . . . it must. I mean . . . the people at church . . . everyone says . . ."

"I know," I said. "Everyone says, 'Forgive and forget.' That's a very old saying, and it's found in most every culture, Myra. But it definitely doesn't come from the Bible. And to tell you the truth, it's not very good advice. You shouldn't forget what happened, Myra. If anything, I want you to *remember*."

Myra just sat there. She obviously did not know what to make of what I was telling her.

"Listen," I said. "Have you ever burned your fingers?" She nodded silently. "And it hurt, didn't it?" She nodded again. "Well, Myra, what would happen if you ever forgot how it hurt, or how you did it?"

"I guess I'd be liable to burn my fingers again," she said. I could see the light of understanding beginning to dawn in her eyes.

"That's exactly right!" I said. "That's one of the things our memory does for us. It helps us learn from the past so that we don't have to repeat painful mistakes.

"Now, Myra," I said, "we've talked a lot about forgiving your father. I've told you how important forgiveness is. But listen to me; I do want you to *forgive* your father, but I do not want you to *forget* what he did. Forgiveness has nothing to do with forgetting. Do you understand? *Forgiveness has nothing to do with forgetting.*"

It is easy to become confused. The Bible says repeatedly that God is able to forgive and forget. For example, God says, "I will forgive their wickedness, and I will never again remember their sins" (Jer. 31:34). The writer of Hebrews repeats this: "I will never again remember their sins and lawless deeds" (Heb. 10:17). But it never says that we are to do the same. We cannot. Only He can. One reason why God can forget is that there is nothing He needs to learn by remembering. There is often a lot of important information that we can learn by remembering, even though we may not want to remember.

I understood how Myra felt. I've felt the same way myself many times. Haven't we all? We want to get rid of the pain of harmful things that have happened to us, and we think that the way to do that is by getting rid of the *memory* of those harmful things. If we can work ourselves around to believing that the hurtful incident never happened, then it can't hurt us anymore.

Or can it? The fact is that very often the harmful effects of past injuries stay with us *whether or not we consciously remember the injuries themselves.* This is why we say that remembering, not forgetting, is the key to forgiveness. Only when we are clear on what has, in fact, happened to us can we deal with it effectively.

We may make connections between current difficulties and painful experiences from our past. The way a friend treats us today may trigger memories of the way our parents or siblings treated us years ago. These memories, in turn, may uncover connections to other past hurts. Many of the problems people bring into counseling stem from things in their past that they needed to remember clearly before they could deal with them.

Take Carol, for example. For as long as she can remember, Carol has felt abandoned and betrayed. She is a very disciplined person, especially in relationships. She avoids giving too much of herself to others. Whenever anyone promises her anything, she immediately begins waiting for that person to fail her.

When she got married, it was only six months before she began to be plagued by fears that her husband was going to leave her. She began to suspect him of seeing other women and accused him of it regularly. If he was even a little bit late getting home, she demanded an accounting of his time. Not surprisingly, her husband did start seeing other women, and he did eventually leave her.

Five years later, Carol met Randy. They fell in love. Randy noticed that she seemed a bit possessive, but he didn't let it bother him—at first. As time went on, though, Carol's mistrustful, clinging behavior asserted itself more and more. Finally, Randy had had enough. "I need a little space!" he yelled at her during an argument. "I need to be able to live life without having to give you a minute-by-minute account."

Carol realized she was again on the verge of destroying a relationship that meant a great deal to her, because of attitudes and actions she could neither understand nor control. That was when she came for help.

As we talked about Carol's family background, she was finally able to recall some of the pain from her childhood. Carol grew up in a family with two working parents. The oldest of three children, she wound up shouldering much of the responsibility for her two brothers. She saw little of her parents except on weekends. Then her parents divorced, and her father moved out of state.

"You know, I've always tried not to think about all that," she said. "Put it all behind me, you know? I guess I just didn't like to think about the miserable childhood I had. But now I see the connection between what happened then and what happens to me now. I've never gotten over being abandoned by my parents, have I?"

That recollection was the beginning of the healing process for Carol. By remembering her past hurts, she began to be able to identify and release negative feelings. Carol will always remember how her parents failed her and damaged her when she was younger. But those injuries won't disable her anymore. Because she was willing to remember them, she was able to overcome them.

You will know that forgiveness has begun
when you recall those who hurt you and feel
the power to wish them well.

LEWIS B. SMEDES, *FORGIVE AND FORGET:*
HEALING THE HURTS WE DON'T DESERVE[1]

That is how forgiveness works. The past is still with us, but now it is truly in the past. It no longer has control over what happens in the present. Its power to dominate our lives is cut off. Forgiving does not mean forgetting, but it does drain the past of its power to hurt us.

A psychologist friend of mine once said, "Those who try to cut themselves off from the past have no future." What he meant was this: When we ignore the past, or try to forget it, its hold on us actually grows stronger. Something from "back then" remains unresolved and interferes with our ability to function in the present.

The Danger of Forgetting

Sandy was extremely distraught, and rightly so. Her father had just been arrested for molesting her eight-year-old daughter. As we talked about her pain at what happened to her daughter, it seemed to me that there was something missing.

I interrupted her and asked, "What aren't you telling me?"

Then the floodgates of her emotions opened and she wept bitterly. Finally she got the words out: "He did the same to me when I was that age!"

When she had regained control of her emotions, I asked her, "How did you deal with what he did to you?"

She told me about seeing a Christian counselor and working through the pain of what her father had done to her, and then she had forgiven him. Then she said, "I thought that since I had forgiven him, I had to act as if it never happened." That's forgetting.

I remained silent, and then she said, "I guess because I forgot, I didn't protect my daughter."

Sometimes it is dangerous to forget. God allows us to remember so that we can learn something in the process. When we forget, we fail to learn what's important.

I often illustrate this point in my seminars by asking the participants to imagine that there is someone in the audience who likes to talk to me, the speaker, but every time he approaches me, he steps on my foot. He gets very anxious about this, but he has discovered that if he steps on my foot and then apologizes, I forgive him, and then his anxiety goes away. Now we can have a nice conversation.

After the fourth time this happens, when he comes up to talk to me, I say, "That's close enough." (You can see I'm a slow learner.)

He looks at me in dismay and says, "Dave, what's wrong?"

I answer, "I remember you. You're the one who likes to step on my foot."

He says back to me, "But I thought you had forgiven me."

I reply, "Oh, I've forgiven you, but I've learned something about you. You like to step on my foot. My foot hurts, and I don't want you to step on my foot again."

Of course, now he is again too anxious to talk, but that's a separate issue. I have remembered this person and protected my foot.

The Unreliability of Memory

The opposite of forgetting can occur when we try too hard to remember things. That can be equally as dangerous as our trying to forget. In the process of trying too hard to remember, research has shown that your mind can create memories that have never happened. Or your mind can add to a memory something that didn't happen. Researchers have found that every time we recall a memory, it can and probably will be different than the previous time we remembered.

One way to think of recording a memory is that it requires adjusting the connections between neurons in our brain. (We have about 100 billion neurons in our brain.) These neurons communicate with each other by sending messages across the narrow gaps between the neurons, called synapses. When we file away in our brain something we want to remember, our brain has to create substances in these synapses to build a "memory path." For years, it was believed that once a memory path was built, it never changed. But more recent studies have shown that recalling a particular memory creates a very similar process in our brain as when we first made the memory. And that is why each time we remember something, there might be some small differences in what we remember compared to the last time.

In other studies, it has been shown that when a person is asked suggestive questions about a memory in a way that causes some doubt in the person about what he or she is remembering, when asked later about the memory, the person often incorporates the ideas that were suggested in the interview.

That's why, in our search to recover the past, we need to be careful. If we have blank spots in our childhood memories, it is important to know that sometimes they will remain blank spots. If we press too hard to remember, we can come up with what we think are recovered memories but are not true memories. They are creations of our imaginative brain. Our healing can only build on what we know for certain.

There are ways that you can help yourself remember factually. You can talk with your siblings to see what they remember, especially your older siblings if you have them. You can look at old photo albums and see if some of the pictures taken during the blank periods in your memory can trigger something. I've had people bring the old photo albums into the counseling room where we look at pictures together. It's interesting to see what someone else will see in a picture of us at a certain age.

Of course, the best way you can proceed when you can't fill in the gaps in your memory is to begin with the things you are doing in the present that are creating pain in your life. Carol began with the behaviors she was struggling with in the present—her jealousy, insecurity and insistence on knowing every move her husband made when he wasn't with her. From that starting point, she worked backward in time to other situations that preceded her marriages where she struggled with similar fears. As she remembered similar emotions in her past, she was able to connect her fears to earlier experiences and eventually filled in enough of the gaps in her memory to focus on her issues with her father.

Trying to Forget

Well-meaning friends often urge us to try to forget bad things that have happened. "Just let it roll off, like water off a duck's back," they say. "The person who hurt you isn't worth wasting your time and energy on, anyway." When people say this, they are in effect saying that our inner pain is trivial. Now, our pain might indeed appear to be of little significance to someone else. But in reality, for us it might run quite deep, especially when we understand the roots of that painful experience. If so, we need to learn how to remember it in a healing way, not try to forget it.

Trying to forget what has happened to us is virtually impossible anyway. It is like trying not to think about something. Try this: For the next 30 seconds, do not think about pink elephants. Think about anything else you like, but no pink elephants.

Could you do it? If you are like many people, you spent the entire 30 seconds saying to yourself, "I will not think about pink elephants. I will not think about pink elephants. I will not think about pink elephants." The result, of course, was that your very effort not to think about pink elephants made it impossible to think about anything else!

Trying to forget works exactly the same way. The more you say to yourself, "I will not remember what my father did to me when I was younger," the more firmly the memory will be planted in your mind.

There is a word for what happens when we try to forget painful memories instead of dealing with them straightforwardly. The word is "denial." When we deny what has happened to us, we do not really forget it, in the sense of getting it out of our system entirely. We just pack it up and store it in our emotional deep freeze. It is like lying to ourselves: By telling ourselves that something bad did not happen—when of course we know that it did—we are only deceiving ourselves.

That self-deception never lasts, and it does not free us from the harmful consequences of the past. Though the painful memories are buried, they are still there, still having their effects on us—as Carol discovered.

"Don't you see?" Judy said. "If I don't remember, then it's as if nothing ever happened. That was how I kept my life together for a long time. I just didn't remember . . ."

"Or *want* to remember," Alice added. "Sometimes it just hurts too much to remember."

"If I persuade myself that it never happened, then I never have to deal with it, do I?" said Carrie. "That was my method for many years."

These three women were members of a group who met weekly for therapy. All eight women came from abusive backgrounds. Four had been sexually abused. All had known the trauma of growing up in seriously unhealthy families. When the group started, six of the eight women had only vague memories of their lives before the age of 10. As they eventually came to recognize, they had employed an unconscious strategy to cope with the pain of the past.

Loss of childhood memories is fairly common among adults who have been severely hurt during their growing-up years. It is, of course, a form of denial. But denial *may* be a helpful process at the time of injury or abuse. Especially when we are young, it may be our only means of coping with a situation we cannot comprehend. "And it worked," as Carrie once said. "We survived, didn't we?" But while denial can be a helpful device during childhood trauma, it becomes a harmful trap later on. As adults, we no longer need to block our memories. Quite the opposite, we often need help to uncover the truth to get in touch with what happened, and to forgive those who caused us pain.

The Process of Integration

Children come into the world with no fear of life and no prejudice against others. Their initial task, as we saw earlier, is to form an attachment with a figure who will make the world a safe and reliable place—usually, the mother. In their undeveloped thinking process, they absolutize things: Everything is either all good or all bad, all right or all wrong. They have no concept of anything but the extremes. Mom, of course, is all good in their view. She is loving and caring, the unfailing source of everything they need and want.

But by the time they reach the crawling stage, they begin to make some very startling discoveries about mom. They begin to realize that the wonderful supplier of all their needs is the same person who did not come to feed them when they were hungry, or did not change their diaper when it was uncomfortable.

Prior to this discovery, the person who did not do these things was "simply out there." There was no identity to the person. Now they begin to make the connection that this unidentified person is the same mom who is so good at taking care of them. They begin to see some badness in mom.

Infants are thus faced with a terrifying dilemma. They desperately need mother to be good in order to keep their scary world safe. How can mom, who is—who must be—all good, be bad? Infants resolve this dilemma by putting the blame—the badness—on themselves.

If the child's emotional development progresses properly, he or she will resolve this dilemma by a process known as *integration*. During this process, the child will begin to put together things that used to seem incompatible to him or her. Mom is not just the "perfect parent personified"; she is good *and* bad, right *and* wrong.

This integration process will continue as long as no trauma or interference comes about. Children will gradually come to understand that parents are human. They are capable of making mistakes, of getting angry, of doing wrong, while remaining capable of loving and caring for them.

What often happens with children from unhealthy families is that the integration process gets short-circuited. They do not develop the ability to see that their parents have both good and bad qualities. They continue to operate from an unconscious belief that things must be either all good or all bad. As we will see in a moment, this results either in outright rejection of the parents or—what is far more likely—unhealthy idealization of the parents.

Black and White?

Children aren't able to recognize the harmful effects stemming from a parent's dysfunctional behavior, especially in relationship to their mother. They attribute the "badness" they experience in their mother to themselves.

This helps illustrate something called "splitting," which is one of the earliest defense mechanisms that develops in children. It is more or less the opposite of integration: the inability to see that good and bad qualities can coexist in the same person.

"It took me a long time to realize that life wasn't just black or white," one man said. "I finally discovered that there are also gray areas. In fact, I learned that life has all kinds of reds and greens and yellows too."

As we have seen, one of the first things we do in life is to divide reality into all good and all bad. If we are able to mature emotionally, we will come to see that life is not so easily categorized. We are able to integrate seemingly contradictory experiences. When we are prevented from maturing emotionally, we continue to force everything into one of two categories: all good or all bad. When our parents are in question, the pressure is almost overwhelming to consider them "all good" despite their problems.

It's not hard to see why, when we look at parents through the eyes of a small child:

- Adults are bigger.
- Adults are smarter.
- Parents have power.
- Parents can hurt children.

If we accept these notions about our parents—and as children, we really have little choice—then we have to conclude that they know what is best for us, and that they are always right. This tendency to always view our parents as all good is called *idealization*.

Idealization often occurs in families that are very religious, especially in those kinds of religious homes that draw very strict boundaries to define acceptable and unacceptable attitudes and behaviors. The high value that is placed on family and on respect for parents makes it almost impossible for children to integrate their parents' failings and weaknesses.

This was made clear to me by the experience of a pastor friend of mine in Atlanta. He was 23 and had just been installed in his first parish. Desiring to get acquainted with his new parishioners, he made appointments to visit all of them in their homes.

One day he visited three sisters, all single, all in their late fifties. They lived together in a large home built by their father. He had died when they were young, and their mother had raised them. She had been dead at least 15 years by the time my pastor friend arrived on the scene. But, as he was to discover, she was still a powerful presence in their lives.

The sisters led the pastor into the living room, which was dominated by a large painting of a middle-aged woman. "That is our mother," one of the sisters said in a hushed voice.

"An absolute saint," said the second sister.

"The perfect mother," added the third.

For a full 40 minutes, the conversation centered around the angelic mother. The young pastor had never encountered anything like it, and he was overwhelmed by their adoration. Yet he couldn't believe that anyone could be quite *that* wonderful.

Later he mentioned his experience to one of the older members of the congregation, who had become a friend and confidant. The man laughed. "Why, their mother was about as mean as a woman could be," he said. "Ran their lives like a dictator. I don't think she ever let them go out on a date or develop any real friendships."

Adult children who have practiced this degree of splitting and idealization tend to be driven by fear. First, there is fear of being abandoned. "I was always afraid my mother was going to leave us," one woman remembered. "When we did something bad, she threatened to walk out and never come back. I remember many afternoons when I ran home from school, afraid that the house would be empty when I got there. She never actually left, but I always feared she would."

Such children also fear loss of control or loss of autonomy. For children who are growing up in a dysfunctional family, control is all-important. It is the only answer to the chaos that surrounds them. The problem, of course, is that none of us can control life completely, and the more we try, the more out of control we feel. But the fear of losing control drives us to try all the harder, despite the suffering and frustration it causes.

Blaming Ourselves

Children need the protection of the adults in their lives, who can love them and help orient them to the world around them. When children grow up in unhealthy homes; when these basic needs are not met; when they are abused, neglected, exploited or deceived, they are damaged and their development is short-circuited.

The blame for all this has to land somewhere. If a child idealizes his parents, the child becomes the only available target. Children grow up thinking *they* are the bad ones. Even if others try to tell them they are good, inwardly they don't believe it. How could it be true? Other people just don't realize how awful they really are. "I have trouble whenever anyone says, 'I love you,'" one woman explained. "In our family, whenever I heard those words, it meant I was about to be taken advantage of."

The normal reaction to these kinds of injury should be anger. But since children in hurtful environments are often forbidden to express anger—or are too young even to realize what is happening to them—they repress their feelings and deny their memories of what has happened.

But even when denial shuts out the source of pain, the feelings of anger, helplessness, despair, suspicion, fear of rejection, abandonment, anxiety and pain are still present. They may find expression in psychological disorders or in such self-destructive behaviors as substance abuse or suicide. When these adult children become parents, they may take revenge on their own children for the mistreatment they received in childhood. Or their unresolved negative emotions may find expression in destructive acts against others, even leading to criminal behavior.

When denial is allowed to continue into adulthood, it opens the door to many problems. The answer to those problems is never to forget. It is remembering that makes healing and freedom possible.

*Not everything that is faced can be changed, but
nothing can be changed until it is faced.*
JAMES BALDWIN

Acceptance

The key to remembering is *acceptance*. We need to accept the reality of what happened to us, so that we can deal with it. One man said that his dad beat him at least twice a week while he was growing up. Later, as an adult out living on his own, he would visit his father and try not to remember the terrible things that had happened in years past. But he couldn't do it. He thought of the places where the beatings had taken place, the belt his dad had used and even the lamp that had fallen and broken during one incident. "Trying not to remember didn't help," he said. "He beat me. It happened."

Accepting the reality of what happened in the past is especially difficult—and especially important—for victims of sexual abuse. One man said, "I kept thinking I must be making this up. My older sister would never have done such things to me." He tried for years to persuade himself that the assaults never happened. But it did not work. In the end he had to say, "She did it. It happened. I can accept that now."

This man accepted the reality of his pain. He learned that there could be no freedom without this acceptance. Forgiveness can occur only after we have acknowledged and accepted that there is something to be forgiven.

We must accept the fact that we hurt. We have suffered because of someone else's actions. What makes it worse is that "someone else" is usually very close to us, someone with whom we have a strong, lasting bond: our parents, our siblings, our spouses, our children, our friends. Occasionally we experience injury from more distant figures, or from some impersonal entity like an organization. The choice is always the same: to accept the reality or to deny it. Denying it—repressing it, pushing it down inside us—only intensifies resentment and stops the healing process.

What has happened to us has happened. Our parents hurt us. Our friends let us down. Our neighbors treated us badly. Our co-workers deceived us. We cannot change those facts. They remain so for all eternity. But with the help of God, we *can* change the *meaning* of those facts. It happens through the process of forgiveness.

In his book *Caring Enough to Confront,* David Augsburger says, "Forgiveness is a journey of many steps." That little sentence sums up much of what I have been saying. As much as we might like forgiveness to be quick and easy, it is a process. It is a journey, which can take many steps. The first step—choosing to forgive, choosing not to hang on to the emotional IOU—is important and should not be overlooked. But the other steps are important, too, and we should not pass over them lightly.

We can learn a great deal from forgiveness. Being hurt by someone only teaches us to protect ourselves and to mistrust others. Forgiveness, however, presents us with a choice as to how to respond. We can brush off what has happened by extending superficial forgiveness, ending up bitter and resentful. Or we can choose the path of true forgiveness and learn lessons along the way that will shape our lives for the better.

If we are going to take God's principles seriously, we will see that forgiveness isn't optional; it is essential. What is optional is whether we choose the quick and easy path of superficial forgiveness, or the harder but more rewarding path of genuine forgiveness.

Many Jewish people celebrate *Kristallnacht* (the Night of Broken Glass) each November, on the anniversary of the night in 1938 when the Nazis smashed the glass in synagogues all over Germany. A few years ago, I attended a *Kristallnacht* service. Among those who spoke were two survivors of the Nazi concentration camps.

The first speaker, a bent-over woman with a deeply lined face, recounted in a calm, controlled voice the terrible inhumanities she had suffered. She cried only when she told how her husband and son had been sent to the gas chambers while she stood by, watching helplessly. As she concluded, she straightened up, looked out at us, and said, "We forgive the Germans. But we can never forget."

I thought to myself, *She understands what forgiveness is all about.* It has nothing to do with forgetting. The power lies in the fact that we forgive *even as we remember.* If we could really forget, we could not forgive. How could we forgive an offense we are not even aware of? The power of forgiveness is that, even in the face of inescapable reality, it liberates us from the inner anger, the resentment, the quest for vengeance that eats away at us and, in the end, will destroy us if we do not forgive.

Key Points to Remember

1. It's not a human characteristic to forgive and forget.

2. It can be dangerous to forget.

3. Memory can be unreliable, so we need to be careful in our remembering.

4. Looking at what's not working in your life today gives you clues about earlier experiences that were hurtful in their effect on you.

5. Remembering can be hurtful, but the goal is acceptance.

Note

1. Lewis B. Smedes, *Forgive and Forget: Healing the Hurts We Don't Deserve* (New York: Harper & Row, 1984).

What's Anger Got to Do with It?

Many people are uncomfortable with anger.
They have been taught that getting angry is always
wrong—that "nice people" don't get angry.
In fact, anger is a normal human reaction to being
hurt. And working through your anger is an
important part of forgiveness.

Would you agree or disagree with the following statements: *Without anger, most forgiveness is superficial. Genuine forgiveness almost always includes anger.*

Long experience in helping people deal with dysfunctional family issues leads me to *agree* with these statements. However, these statements bother many people. They tend to have a certain amount of mistrust concerning anger and are especially uncomfortable connecting it with something like forgiveness. But the fact is that anger and forgiveness tend to be intimately connected. In most cases, we cannot truly forgive until we have dealt with our anger. To put it another way, working through anger is often a crucial step in the process of forgiveness.

A lot of confusing ideas circulate about anger. Many of us were brought up to believe that all anger is wrong, even sinful. But anger is a fact of life. It happens to us. We experience it. What do we do then? Many of us play word games with it. We say we are "a little irritated" or "out of sorts" or "a bit upset." We go to great lengths to avoid coming right out and saying, "I'm just plain *mad*."

But the fact is, we often *are* just plain mad, and there is not necessarily anything wrong with that. The emotion of anger, in and of itself, is not wrong. Let me say that again, to make sure you get it: The emotion of anger, in and of itself, is not wrong. It just *is*. It is part of the "standard equipment" that comes with being a human being. It's there to help protect us when we are threatened. It is what we *do* with our anger that makes it either right or wrong, good or bad, healthy or unhealthy.

We can *use* our anger wrongly, or *express* it in unhealthy ways. A simple example is when we fly off the handle at someone we love without good cause. Unhealthy anger separates us from people we love and want to be with.

But we can also use our anger for healthy purposes. For example, anger can energize us to overcome some challenge or obstacle. Who among us has not had the experience of getting good and mad at some stubborn problem, and finding that the energy produced by that anger gets us over the hump?

> *Healthy anger drives us to do something to change what makes us angry; anger can energize us to make things better. Hate does not want to change things for the better; it wants to make things worse.*
> LEWIS B. SMEDES, *FORGIVE AND FORGET: HEALING THE HURTS WE DON'T DESERVE*[1]

We may have trouble accepting the notion that anger is a normal, inevitable part of life. We have been carefully taught that anger is always wrong, that nice people don't get angry.

Nonsense. The simple fact of the matter is that nice people get angry all the time. The problem is that these folks often don't *realize* that they are angry, or they don't know what to *do* with their anger. We'll talk more about those problems as we go along.

But to repeat what we said before: Anger is not wrong, in and of itself. The capacity to feel and express anger is part of what it

means to be a healthy human being. When we run across someone who seems to have lost the ability to feel or express anger, or
who has become expert at stuffing his or her anger deep inside, we
recognize that as a problem, not as a virtue.

Anger as a Virtue

Good people get angry. Even Jesus did. Listen to this passage from
the Gospel of Mark:

> Jesus went into the synagogue again and noticed a man
> with a deformed hand. Since it was the Sabbath, Jesus' en-
> emies watched him closely. If he healed the man's hand,
> they planned to accuse him of working on the Sabbath.
>
> Jesus said to the man with the deformed hand, "Come
> and stand in front of everyone." Then he turned to his crit-
> ics and asked. "Does the law permit good deeds on the
> Sabbath, or is it a day for doing evil? Is this a day to save
> life or to destroy it?" But they wouldn't answer him.
>
> He looked around at them angrily and was deeply sad-
> dened by their hard hearts. Then he said to the man, "Hold
> out your hand." So the man held out his hand, and it was
> restored! At once the Pharisees went away and met with the
> supporters of Herod to plot how to kill Jesus (Mark 3:1-6).

Here we find Jesus confronting a crippled man who wants to
be healed. It's unbelievable that a group of religious leaders do not
want Jesus to heal him because, according to their understanding
of God's law, it is the wrong day of the week. We see Jesus responding to the situation with the full range of human emotion. Surely
He must have felt compassion toward the man with the withered
hand. But what did He feel toward the religious leaders? It says He
was "deeply saddened by their hard hearts." It also says that He
looked at them in *anger*.

Here again, we see healthy anger serving a good purpose. Jesus uses it to communicate His displeasure to the religious leaders.

He also seems to use it to energize Himself to push past their opposition and heal the man.

Paul also wrote some helpful things about anger. Much of the content of his letters in the New Testament has to do with wisdom for daily living. In a letter to the church at Ephesus, Paul makes the point that all Christians belong, in some sense, to one people. He then goes on to give practical advice on how to live together as part of a united family, including these words: "So stop telling lies. Let us tell our neighbors the truth, for we are all parts of the same body. And 'don't sin by letting anger control you.' Don't let the sun go down while you are still angry, for anger gives a foothold to the devil" (Eph. 4:25-27).

Notice the line, "don't sin by letting anger control you." That line can also be translated, "Be angry, but do not sin." Paul seems to be saying:

- There is a difference between "anger" and "sin."
- It is possible to be angry *without* sinning.
- There are times when it is actually *right* for us to be angry, so long as we do not sin in doing so.
- Some anger can be sinful, and some anger is not sinful.

The line, "don't sin by letting anger control you," is actually a quotation from the psalms: "Don't sin by letting anger control you. Think about it overnight and remain silent" (Ps. 4:4).

The image of lying on our beds at night, quietly searching our hearts, helps to give meaning to Paul's warning: "Do not let the sun go down on your anger." On the one hand, we can take this literally. Paul warns that anger is a destructive force, both in terms of our spiritual health and in terms of our relationships, and we should make dealing with it a priority. If possible, we should try to clear up whatever is standing between us and the person with whom we are angry. That is not always possible, of course. Perhaps you have seen the cartoon of the couple dozing off in the marriage counselor's office? The husband lifts up his head and, through bloodshot eyes, says, "Well, you told us not to go to bed angry, so we haven't slept for a week."

If we cannot resolve our anger at the interpersonal level, we should at least deal with it in terms of our own emotions, getting it out into the open so that the poison does not fester within us. I've presented in earlier chapters how to "express" feelings in this sense: writing your feelings down, sharing them with a friend, even vocalizing them to yourself.

> *Resentment is like a poison we carry around inside us with the hope that when we get the chance we can deposit it where it will harm another who has injured us. The fact is that we carry this poison at extreme risk to ourselves.*
>
> BERT GHEZZI, *THE ANGRY CHRISTIAN*[2]

This helps us grasp another, somewhat more figurative, understanding of Paul's words. We can hear him saying, "Do not let your anger go into the darkness—into that place where you cannot see it, or feel it or even acknowledge its existence." We have already seen how harmful it can be to repress our feelings; anger can be one of the most harmful feelings to repress. It is like an acid that eats away at us from the inside.

Anger that is left unresolved or buried in the darkness of denial takes root and produces bitterness and resentment. The longer we postpone dealing with anger, the more bitterness and resentment it engenders, and the harder it becomes for us to get in touch with its existence and purge it from our hearts. Once we are aware that we are angry, we know immediately that we must at least begin the process of forgiveness and keep our anger in the daylight where we can deal with it.

Angry? Me?

One of the main problems posed by anger is that we sometimes do not even realize that we *are* angry. This is especially true with people who believe that anger is always wrong or sinful. They do not even let themselves become aware that they are experiencing anger. Instead they repress it, give it a different name or pretend it doesn't exist.

Over lunch in the company cafeteria, John listened as Brian told him about a situation that happened in his office that morning. Brian's boss had walked in, slammed the door behind him and started barking out questions and accusations.

"Sounds like a bad scene," John said, shaking his head. "What did you say?"

"Say? I didn't say anything." Brian shrugged. "I couldn't get a word in edgewise. I was trying to explain to him what happened, but it was obvious he didn't really want to listen. He just wanted to unload."

"So you got it cleared up?" John asked.

"Well, he eventually settled down and I was able to explain a little bit," Brian said. "He only had about half the story and even most of that was inaccurate. But it didn't really matter. Like I said, he just wanted to unload on someone. I just happened to be the closest person. Tough luck for me."

"So how do you feel now?" John asked.

"Well . . . okay, I guess," Brian sighed. "I was pretty ticked off this morning. But it's over and done with now, I guess. I've forgiven him."

Brian started to talk about something else, but John put up his hand. "Hold on a second," he said. "What do you mean, you've forgiven him? You don't sound like you've forgiven him. In fact, you still sound pretty angry to me."

Brian looked at him with a puzzled expression. "I do? I mean, I was angry at first, but . . ."

"Just listen to you," John said. "Your voice, the expression on your face, even the way you're sitting—you seem to me like you're still angry, and that's okay."

"I guess you're right. I am still upset," Brian admitted. "A lot of what he said really got to me. I mean, I knew he had the facts wrong, and there was nothing I could do about it. But as I said, it's over now, so I just need to forgive and move on."

John smiled. "But that's just my point, Brian. You are getting ahead of yourself. You need to process the anger and hurt so the forgiveness is real." It took his friend John to point out that Brian was still angry, and that not processing his anger would limit his ability to really forgive and move on. This is not an uncommon scenario. Sometimes we need to have our anger pointed out to us, whether by a friend or a counselor.

Once, between sessions at a conference, I overheard one of the leaders yell at another person in obvious anger. His voice was strident and his words were harsh. It was an unpleasant exchange to listen to—never mind being on the receiving end of it!

Later that day, I had a chance to talk to the man who had done the yelling. I mentioned that I overheard what had happened. "Oh, that," he said. "It was just one of those things that happens sometimes. No big deal."

No big deal? I thought to myself. *It sure sounded like a big deal to me.* "Tell me," I said, "what were you feeling while you were . . . uh . . . *talking* to him?"

"Feeling?" he said, looking at me quizzically. "I don't know. I wasn't feeling anything. There were some things I needed to say to him, and . . ."

"Didn't you feel angry?" I interrupted.

"Oh, no," he said quickly. "No, not at all. I wasn't angry. I was just . . ." he let the sentence trail off.

As we talked, it became clear to me that he was convinced that anger was bad. Because of this, he could not admit to me, or even to himself, that he had been angry. I believe he was utterly sincere in what he was saying to me. Yet, I had seen a man whose face was flushed, whose voice thundered, whose hands trembled and whose words could have peeled paint off the walls. He was a classic case of someone *experiencing* anger without being able to *acknowledge* it.

Vic had come to see me about a long-standing depression he suffered from. He had been to a therapist several times, trying to break the hold it had on him, but without much success.

Somehow, we got to talking about his father, who had died when Vic was only 10 years old. Vic could not talk about his father without crying, even though he had died almost 30 years earlier. It seemed clear that his dad's death was somehow connected to his depression.

Perhaps the most damaging consequence of being shame-based is that we don't know how depressed and angry we really are. We don't actually feel our unresolved grief. Our false self and ego defenses keep us from experiencing it. Paradoxically, the very defenses that allowed us to survive our childhood trauma have now become barriers to our growth.

JOHN BRADSHAW,
HEALING THE SHAME THAT BINDS YOU[3]

At one point, I asked Vic if he had ever been angry with his father for dying. He looked at me with a shocked expression, as if I had violated something sacred. "Angry?" he said. "How could I be angry with him? He didn't die on purpose."

I agreed, but went on to explain that much of the grieving process has to do with working through anger, including anger at the deceased one for leaving. Vic listened intently for a while, then dismissed the subject with a wave of the hand, saying he couldn't see any connection between his depression and anger.

Several sessions later, I brought up the subject again. This time Vic admitted that what I had said bothered him. If he really thought about it, maybe there *was* a little anger there after all. But not at his dad. At the doctors, maybe, or even at God. But not Dad!

I decided to try another tack. "Let me ask you something, Vic," I said. "What do you think you lost because of your dad dying while you were so young?" He thought for a while. Then he began listing a number of things he had missed out on by not having had a father: someone to watch his Little League games, someone to help him with his homework, someone to tell him about girls, someone to guide him through major life decisions, and so on. Vic went on for quite some time.

When he finished, I quietly commented, "You know, I think I'd be angry at someone who took all those things away from me, even if he didn't mean to do it." I could see the realization slowly begin to dawn in Vic's eyes.

Later, after Vic had been able to identity some of the anger he held toward his father, he was able to talk about why it was so hard for him to think of being angry with him. Like many people, Vic simply did not know how to deal with anger, either his own or other people's. It made him uncomfortable. So he just pretended that it didn't exist. As we have already seen, ignoring strong emotions doesn't make them go away; it just drives them deeper inside where they continue to affect us without our consciously realizing it.

It was no surprise, then, that even in his adult life, Vic turned out to have a problem with anger. Whenever things went wrong, it would send him off on a rampage that left him feeling embarrassed and guilty. I explained to him that self-control in the emotional area is one of the things that a father might teach a young boy. "Another thing I missed out on," he said.

Vic had never entertained the notion of needing to forgive his dad for anything. He had idealized him to the point that his dad was a virtual saint in his eyes. To even think of being angry at Dad was preposterous. To think of him needing to be forgiven for anything was inconceivable.

Coming to grips with his anger not only gave Vic an awareness of some important losses he had sustained in life, but it also set the stage for him to work through some important forgiveness regarding his father. And not because his father had, in the strict sense, done anything wrong. Vic was quite right in saying that it wasn't his dad's fault that he died. But even without realizing it, Vic was still holding some IOUs against his father—debts he needed to cancel for the sake of his own health.

Anger as Reaction, Anger as Response

Anger is one of those concepts that get more confusing the longer you study it. One reason is that we use the word in such a variety of contexts. I get angry over the car not starting, angry with my father for dying 30 years ago, angry at racial injustice, angry because there are homeless people in a land as prosperous as ours.

I like to think of anger in two basic ways: as *reaction* and as *response*.

Reaction is what happens in us automatically, or instinctively, in answer to some stimulus. This is the way we tend to think of anger as an emotion. Someone says something that hurts us, or does something that harms us, and the emotion of anger wells up inside us. We don't plan it or think about it, and we can't prevent it. It just happens.

Response is what we *decide* to do in response to some stimulus. It is, at least to some degree, conscious and deliberate. Our reactions happen to us, but we choose our responses.

Obviously, the same stimulus can give rise to both a reaction and a response. To take a simple example, let's say you come along and, for no apparent reason, slap me in the face. Immediately, I experience a reaction: My face flushes and my muscles tense up. I begin to snap, "Why, you . . ."

Then I stop and reflect on what happened. I take note of my reaction. I also take note of the context in which you did what you did. Maybe there was some good reason why you did it, or some good reason why I should let it pass. I may decide that the appropriate response is to simply turn and walk away. Or I may decide that the appropriate response is to confront you about your behavior.

If I choose the latter response, we would probably say that I am expressing anger rather than patience. The point is simply to note the difference between reaction—what just happens—and response—what I choose to do.

Anger is a normal human reaction to such experiences as pain, fear and frustration. When someone does something against us—whether intentional or not—anger is likely to be one of our first and strongest reactions.

It often helps to take a closer look at what goes on inside us when we have an anger reaction. (Usually, of course, we have to do this well after the fact, when we've cooled down a bit!) For example, suppose I have been teaching a seminar. During the discussion period someone named Herb mentions that he disagrees with my views on anger. He is utterly convinced that anger is always wrong. In answer, I review for him the points I have been advancing here: that anger is inherently neither good nor bad, merely a fact of life; it is our *response* that makes it either good or bad.

"Well, there you go again, Dave," Herb snaps. "You're the expert. You're always right and everyone else is always wrong. You think you're so smart. Well, actually you're overbearing, pompous and obnoxious."

What do you suppose is going on inside me as Herb is speaking? First, of course, I recognize that I am being insulted. This comes as a shock. I see myself as being utterly pristine, acting from the purest of motives, guilty of nothing but being who I am and saying what I honestly believe. Overbearing? Pompous? *Me?*

Along with this comes the realization that Herb doesn't regard me as being valuable enough to deserve better treatment. If he respected me, he wouldn't talk to me like this in front of other people. The message I get is, "You don't count, Dave."

Can you imagine that by this point I am beginning to experience an anger reaction?

Now, I may be able to fend off that reaction. If my self-esteem is in good shape, and if I have had a good night's sleep, I may be able to simply say to myself, *Well, that's just not true. I'm not any of those bad things Herb says I am. He just has an inaccurate perception of me as a person.* If so, I may well short-circuit the anger.

But perhaps I'm not so confident, or maybe my defenses are down for some reason—maybe I'm feeling tired or hungry or I'm not feeling well. I might be tempted to believe the things Herb said. *Maybe I only got what I deserve,* I might think to myself. But even if I do, my next thought is likely to be, *How dare he say that in front of all these people!* Now my anger is giving birth to resentment.

Or I may simply reject Herb and his message. *That's absurd. He has no right to say those things! Why, I ought to . . .* Now my anger is in full flight.

Why? Because Herb has touched something significant. He has managed to get down to my inner self, to the core of my being. He has, to use the popular expression, pushed my button.

Call Waiting

All this helps us understand the anatomy of a reaction. But the only reason to understand our *reactions* is in order to help us select an appropriate *response*. Let's suppose you are in a situation where your button has been pushed and your anger reaction is in full swing. What are you to *do* with your anger? There are four basic responses:

1. You Can Repress the Emotion

Some people can be insulted, cursed, yelled at—all but stomped on—and seem to respond to it like a stone. At the conscious level, at least, they simply don't feel anger. They have learned, probably from a young age, that it isn't safe—or simply doesn't pay—to allow themselves to experience the emotion of anger. So when it begins to rise up in them, they push it back down. They *repress* it.

Repressed anger is similar to the call waiting feature on the telephone. With call waiting, you can talk to one person on the phone and receive a beep alert that another call is trying to get through. You can continue with your current conversation and try to ignore the second call. But the periodic beep reminds you that the call is there, and it gets increasingly difficult to ignore.

Repressed anger is like that. You can go on with your life as if it weren't there, trying to ignore it—but it is there. Until something is done with it, it won't go away. It will find ways to "leak out" in the form of depression, bitterness, mistrust, self-pity, anxiety, being critical, and so on.

In recent years, doctors have learned that repressed anger can even contribute to physical disorders. Cancer researchers have profiled what they call the "typical cancer personality," traits that people with cancer seem to exhibit to an unusually consistent degree as compared with other people. There are four main components:

1. Poor self-image
2. Inability to form or maintain long-term relationships
3. Tendency to self-pity
4. Tendency to hold resentment and inability to forgive[4]

The fourth component relates directly to repressed anger. Much of the work done by cancer therapists has to do with helping patients bring their anger out into the open where it can be worked on and processed. Many patients who did so experienced remarkable remissions of their disease.

Repressed anger is like steam building up in a pressure cooker. A pressure cooker has a main valve and a safety valve. If we continue to repress our anger while trying to keep all the valves shut, eventually the lid will blow off! The pressure can build for only so long before it has to be released. The steam *will* come out. The only questions are how? and when?—and who gets hurt when the lid blows?

2. You Can Vent Your Anger

Years ago, people recognized the dangers of repressing anger, and in response they have pushed the pendulum all the way to the other side. "Anger," they said, "must be fully and freely expressed the instant it appears. Don't delay. Don't hold back. Be 'authentic' with your feelings."

Perhaps you have had the misfortune of being around people who have taken this approach to the limit. They are constantly unloading on those around them. If they are sad, they spread gloom everywhere. If they are frightened, they panic everyone else. And if they are angry, look out! A lot of innocent bystanders have been hit by a full dose of someone else's angry authenticity. They can tell you it's no fun.

Authenticity may be well and good in its place, but running around yelling, cursing and being destructive is no solution to anger. These ways of venting our anger may make us feel better, at least for the moment, but they ruin relationships, and in time they undermine our own emotional health.

I remember one man who came to our clinic. He said, "Whenever I get angry, I just haul off and yell at whoever is handy," he said defiantly. "I always feel so much better afterward—you know, like a load has been taken off me."

His problem? "The reason I need to talk to you," he said, "is that I don't have any friends. Everybody seems to act—I don't know, like they're *afraid* of me. They say they don't like being around me." Small wonder!

3. You Can Feel Your Anger but Not Express It Right Away

"Fools vent their anger, but the wise quietly hold it back" (Prov. 29:11). This means that you let yourself experience your anger— you don't repress it—but you also choose to handle it in productive and healthy ways. In other words, you decide to *respond* rather than *react*. It is as if you say to yourself, "Yes, I'm angry, but I'm not going to do anything until I've had a chance to think it over."

When a person is angry, he or she usually doesn't see things clearly. We would all do well to ask for grace to help us remain calm until we can be more objective. The old adage of "counting to 10" also fits here (though sometimes we may feel the need to count to a million!).

4. You Can Learn to Confess Your Anger to Someone You Trust

First of all, let's get clear about the word "confess." At root, it simply means "to say the same as," or "to give accurate verbal expression to what is real." In this sense, it doesn't carry the connotation of "admitting guilt." It simply means you are being candid and honest about what is going on.

In terms of your emotions, confessing your anger means that you share openly and honestly about what is going on inside you. "I'm really feeling angry right now about . . ." Or, "When she said that to me, I got so mad I just wanted to . . ." The goal is to get the feelings out on the table, where you can understand them more clearly and decide how best to respond to them. "When it first happened, I felt like (slugging him, screaming at him, running away). But now I can see that the best thing to do is . . ."

Support Systems

The healthy way to express anger points to the importance of having a support system of some caring people in your life—people that you can trust and with whom you can be open. Anger that is carried alone will often wind up getting repressed, and it will reinforce your sense of isolation. Talking out your feelings with someone else helps you process your feelings in healthy ways.

Response number 4 was the approach that Vic opted for. He handled his anger in the context of a relationship of trust. He was able to let himself feel anger at the loss he had sustained, which opened the door to a more comprehensive grieving process.

Four Basic Responses to an Anger Reaction

1. You can repress the emotion. Watch out! Repressed emotions create pressure that will eventually result in an explosion.

2. You can vent your anger. "Don't delay. Don't hold back. Be 'authentic' with your feelings!" Following such advice can provide momentary relief, but it eventually ruins relationships and undermines your own emotional health.

3. You can feel your anger but decide not to express it right away. Often it pays to "count to 10." This strategy gives you the space to respond rather than react.

4. You can learn to confess your anger to someone you trust. The goal is to understand your feelings so that you can decide how best to respond to them.

In the beginning, Vic made use of the third option, where he felt the anger but chose to remain in control of his response. That in itself was new for him. Usually, whenever Vic felt anger, his normal course of action was to attack, which only compounded his problems. Eventually he decided to talk about his anger with a trusted third party. This helped him work through his anger fruitfully. In his case, that was a crucial first step in embarking on the process of forgiveness.

Remember Herb, the man in the hypothetical example, who insulted me in front of a room full of people? In that story, I contemplated a number of responses, both internal and external, to that situation. Perhaps the healthiest response I could make would be to say, "Okay, Herb's angry right now. I don't know exactly why. But I *do* know I can't help the situation by matching his anger with my own. For now I'll just keep my peace. Later, I can ask someone to help me sort out what was going on with Herb and what I needed to do with him."

Of course, it's a lot easier to say these things than to actually do them. Options 1 and 2 are a lot easier and don't require much self-control. But the consequences are almost always negative, only adding fuel to a fire in someone else that is already ablaze.

KEY POINTS TO REMEMBER

1. Dealing with the major hurts in your past without feeling the anger ends up being excusing, not forgiving.

2. Anger is a valid emotion—it's what you do with it that makes it good or bad.

3. We sin when we let anger control us.

4. Repressing anger or venting anger works against your healing.

5. Confessing your anger to a trusted friend is a healthy way to handle anger.

Notes

1. Lewis B. Smedes, *Forgive and Forget: Healing the Hurts We Don't Deserve* (New York: Harper & Row, 1984), p. 21.

2. Bert Ghezzi, *The Angry Christian* (Ann Arbor, MI: Servant Publications, 1980), p. 99.

3. John Bradshaw, *Healing the Shame that Binds You* (Deerfield Beach, FL: Health Communications, Inc., 1988), p. 137.

4. This formulation is taken from Carl Simonton, M.D., Stephanie Matthews-Simonton and James L. Creighton, *Getting Well Again* (New York: Bantam Books, 1978).

The Blame Game

People who grew up in dysfunctional families often feel that everything that goes wrong in the world is their fault. Understanding how you have been victimized is important. So is learning to take responsibility for your life, and not blaming all of your problems on others.

"If only she would get what she deserves."

I was taken aback by the bitterness in Meg's voice as she virtually spat out these harsh words. The "she" Meg was referring to was her twin sister, Martha. The two sisters had not been on speaking terms for more than 30 years. It all went back to the time when they were both single. They were young, attractive and vivacious, with many potential boyfriends. Meg had dated a young man named Jeff. She had gotten quite serious about him. She was shocked then, when Jeff abruptly broke off their relationship and started seeing her sister, Martha. Meg flew into a rage at her sister for luring her man away.

Jeff and Martha eventually got married. Martha would have liked for Meg to serve as her maid of honor, but Meg refused. In fact, Meg wouldn't even come to the wedding. Ever since, she has blamed every misfortune, every disappointment and every setback in life on her sister. "She stole the only man I ever loved," was Meg's constant refrain for 30 years.

I knew Meg for many years. She was grouchy and cantankerous, not an easy person to like. I tried many times to help her see how fruitless it was to blame all her woes on something that happened so many years before. But it never made a dent in her conviction that Martha was the cause of all her problems. "When she confesses to what she did and apologizes for ruining my life, then I'll forgive her," Meg said. Somehow she did not see that this demand was inconsistent with her refusal to allow Martha even to speak with her. She seemed incapable of viewing life except through the lens of what she saw as her sister's act of treachery.

When I last saw her, Meg was in the hospital dying of pancreatic cancer. She flatly refused to allow her sister to visit her. "I wish Martha could slowly drown for all the suffering she's caused me," Meg said. "If only she would get what she deserves."

Martha never came to the hospital, but she did come to the funeral. "I tried so many times to make things right with Meg," she told me. "You know, I probably *did* steal Jeff away from her. It was a game we played for years, flirting with each other's boyfriends. We both did it. But it stopped being a game when I truly fell in love with Jeff. Meg hated me ever since. I guess she felt I had finally won the game once and for all. She would tell anyone who'd listen to her that I didn't really love Jeff, and she did."

How many others are there like Meg, consumed with an impossible demand for vengeance? We all know the saying "an eye for an eye; a tooth for a tooth." Did you know it comes from the Bible? Originally, it was God's way of *limiting* the vengeance that people took on one another. In Old Testament times it was not uncommon for people to extract a *life* in payment for even a minor injury. But in time, God introduced the standard of mercy, not the standard of vengeance, as the guiding principle in our relationships.

Still, the only way that many people deal with an offense is to punish the offender. Interestingly, even when the guilty parties have been punished, those who have been wronged still have no peace. The memory of the offense does not go away. That tortured memory remains the source of anguish and turmoil. Bitterness and resentment linger; anger continues to rage.

Sometimes those who have been hurt will take out their frustration on others without even realizing they are doing it. They become irritable and insulting. Their friends find them increasingly difficult to get along with—while they still have friends. In the end their resentment destroys their own freedom. They become incapable of *not* acting spitefully, so thoroughly has the poison of resentment infiltrated their system. That is the inevitable outcome of the blame game: Those who play it *always* end up losers.

Have you ever noticed that it's fun to blame others? That's one of the reasons why we do it. If we're honest with ourselves, most of us will admit that we get a kind of perverse pleasure out of blaming others. We may even share our "somebody done me wrong" tale with others whom we know we can count on to add their understanding and sympathy. In effect, we throw a pity party, focusing on our pain and our resentment, having a fun time in a twisted sort of way.

Sometimes we blame others as a cover-up for fear—fear of punishment, embarrassment, responsibility and the like. Self-protection is a strong drive in all of us.

At the most basic level, our tendency to blame others probably stems from our fundamental conviction that we ourselves are blameless. Isn't that right? We might never come out and say it, but deep in our heart we know we are just, honorable and upright. When things go wrong, it *must* be someone else's fault. Surely it couldn't be ours!

I regularly see an interesting phenomenon occur among adults who were abused as children. They experience an overwhelming need to cast blame *somewhere*. Because of the dynamics of childhood—where adults were bigger and more powerful, and therefore perceived as "always right"—abuse victims invariably place the blame on themselves.

It's not just because the parents were bigger and more powerful. There is another reason why we as adults often blame ourselves for the bad things that have happened to us. As toddlers, we believe we are omnipotent. One child specialist once said that it was good that toddlers have little bodies, or else the planet would be in trouble. At this stage of life, the world revolves around them. If I am a bad boy or girl today, it's my fault that it rains tomorrow and forces us to cancel the picnic we planned. We also see this in pre-school-age children whose parents are divorcing. The children are convinced it is their fault—that they were so bad in some way, that they are the ones causing the parents to divorce. So if we are injured in some way emotionally in those early years, it's natural that we blame ourselves.

I was working with Gina on her molestation by her older brother between the ages of five and eight. When Gina was eight, the parents found out and put an end to it but didn't go any further to get help. As Gina talked in our counseling sessions about what had happened, she was very obviously blaming herself for what her brother had done to her. I kept trying to explain to her how young children think the world revolves around them, and therefore everything is somehow their fault.

As hard as I tried to explain this, it fell on deaf ears. Gina was convinced that it was her fault. Finally, I stopped explaining and did what I should have done earlier. I said, "Tell me how it was your fault."

She waited a while, and then she said, "I believe I had danced provocatively in front of him. I enticed him."

We talked a bit about what she had just said, and then I said to her, "Please, a five-year-old child doesn't even know that word exists, let alone what it means. You could not have done that at that age." Gradually, Gina was able to put the blame where it belonged. It was her brother who bore the responsibility, as the older one, for what had happened.

Soon, adults who were abused as children start accepting the fact that they were only children—innocent, unable to either choose or prevent the things that were happening to them. "For the first time I realized that I wasn't to blame for all the problems that existed in the world," one woman said. "I felt I *had* to blame *someone*. I couldn't blame the adults, because after all, they were *adults*. So the only one left to blame was me."

Once this realization hits, they often start blaming others with a vengeance. Some are simply programmed to blame others for everything. One man named Jerry remembers growing up in a family where *everything* was regarded as someone else's fault. He can remember times when they hoped for a sunny day and it rained. His father would say, "Even God is against us today." Jerry grew up very confused about the matter of responsibility. If he didn't bring about the wrong, then he had to point an accusing finger at someone else.

A more mature understanding of the world tells us that sometimes things just don't work out the way we hoped they would. There are disappointments, unexpected developments and changes in plans that are no one's fault in particular. To paraphrase the popular bumper sticker, "Stuff Just Happens." Being able to accept this reality without always having to point the finger of blame is an important component of personal maturity and emotional health.

The Path of Bitterness

Face it: We want to blame others. When we have been hurt—or *think* we have—something in us wants to place the blame somewhere (usually on someone else). But the more we blame, the farther we walk down the dangerous path of bitterness. That path never leads us to health and happiness, only to deeper distress. Eventually we end up in a pity party, which is expressed in the proverb that says, "Each heart knows its own bitterness, and no one else can fully share its joy" (Prov. 14:10)—the strange "joy" of bitterness.

Some time ago, I came across a story that shows how tragic it can be to walk down the path of bitterness:

> Leonard Goldenson's gentlemanly manner running ABC is well chronicled. Not so well known is his feud with Frank Sinatra. In *Beating the Odds,* Goldenson tells his side.
>
> "Frank's career was in the doldrums. He'd just finished *From Here to Eternity,* but it was months away from release. Nobody yet knew it was going to be the smash hit that would restore Sinatra to superstardom.
>
> "I said, 'Frank, do you have any money?'

"He said 'no.' I said, 'I want you on ABC.' Eventually we agreed to form a production company together. I thought a musical variety show hosted by Sinatra held great promise."

Eternity was a smash, earning Sinatra an Oscar. He lost interest in the TV project, and it faltered. Goldenson flew to Las Vegas to see him about doing specials. For three days Goldenson waited to see him. Then, he had had enough.

"I wrote Sinatra a letter in longhand. 'Never in my life have I experienced such treatment,' I said. 'I have no respect for anyone who lacks the character to appear for an appointment. When you were down on your luck and had no money, we went out of our way to make a capital gain for you. . . . I want nothing further to do with you.' "[1]

The two men never spoke again after the incident in 1954. It would seem from this account that Leonard Goldenson was an intensely bitter man, at least as far as Frank Sinatra was concerned. He obviously blamed Sinatra for a missed opportunity. Now, let's suppose that Sinatra had called Goldenson on the phone one day and said, "You know, Leonard, you're right. It was wrong of me to do what I did." Would Goldenson have felt vindicated? Perhaps. Would that brief moment of satisfaction have been worth decades of blaming and bitterness? I doubt it.

This is the who-started-it game, the search for a beginning of a sequence, where the aim is to proclaim which person is to blame for the behavior of both. But we know that this interaction is really a circular dance in which the behavior of one partner maintains and provokes the behavior of the other. The circular dance has no beginning and no end. In the final analysis, it matters little who started it. The question of greater significance is: "How do we break out of it?"

HARRIET LERNER, *THE DANCE OF ANGER*[2]

The Path of Forgiveness

A lot of psychologist jokes focus on shifting the blame for all our problems to someone else—usually to Mom. I sometimes tell people, "If you want to play the blame game, I can move you through it real quick. Do you want to know why you have the problems you have? Because of your mother. And why do you suppose your mother treated you so badly? Because of *her* mother. And what was *her* mother's problem? Why, her mother before her. And why would sweet little old granny do such a thing? Why, her mother, of course."

Do you see where this leads? Eventually, we get all the way back to Adam. God asks him, "Why did you do this horrible thing?" And Adam looks around and doesn't have a mother to blame, but he has a woman. So he says to God, "Well, it was that woman, who by the way, you made. She made me do it." He not only blamed Eve, but he also put part of the blame on God as well.

Now God turns to Eve and asks the same question: "Why did you do this horrible thing?" Eve looked around, and there was no mother, and no other woman to blame. And then she remembered: "It was that serpent, who you made, God. He made me do it." Eve shirked her own responsibility as well. But she could blame the serpent. So now we can see where the blame game takes us—the devil makes us do the bad things. If we believe in sin, we know that the fault lies with the devil. Years ago, comedian Flip Wilson used to tell us that "the devil made me do it."

But to blame it on sin, or on the devil, doesn't really help us. In other words, the blame game leads nowhere. All it does is prove that we are *all* flawed, imperfect people living in a flawed, imperfect world where "stuff happens." So why bother playing it at all? Why not get off the path of bitterness and get on the path of forgiveness? Instead of blaming, let's resolve the issues. Let's do the work of forgiving.

Playing the blame game just gets in the way of resolving our problems and moving past them. It keeps us mired in them forever. *Blaming other people for our problems doesn't solve our problems, even if we're right.* Think about it: As long as our energies are absorbed with blaming another person, we are really under that person's control.

The image of that person becomes the focal point of our whole life. The hurt doesn't go away just because we figure out who the "villain" is. The hurt goes away only when we work through the process of forgiveness.

Some people are blamers without realizing it. They *think* they are taking appropriate responsibility for their actions, but by attaching "stingers" to their words, "I was wrong" turns into "It's all your fault." For example:

"Honey, I'm sorry I yelled at you last night," a husband said. "I'm also sorry you didn't get supper on the table when I asked you to."

One of the ways to spot an unconscious blamer is when "you" statements creep into "I" statements.

"I feel bad today because you . . ."

"I wouldn't have said what I said if you hadn't . . ."

"I wouldn't have wrecked the car if you had been ready on time so I didn't have to speed to get there."

An interesting twist on this is what happens when we are clearly in the wrong, recognize it and still blame the other person for our actions. "I guess I shouldn't have done it. But he really had it coming. He thinks he's so superior to everyone else." Or, "I shouldn't have treated him that way. But he's such a jerk! Everyone says so."

This is nothing more than rationalizing our misbehavior by claiming that the other person *deserved* to be treated badly on general principles. But it is not up to us to decide what others "deserve." Our job is to take responsibility for our own actions.

A pastor friend of mine told me of an experience he had several years ago. He was invited to join a dozen other ministers for a day-long retreat. At one point during their discussions, my friend—without any conscious thought of offending anyone—said something that deeply hurt one of the other ministers named Dan. It was immediately obvious what had happened; Dan's face flushed and his body stiffened.

A few minutes later, during a coffee break, my friend went up to Dan and said, "Look, I'm really sorry if what I said offended you . . ."

"*If* you offended me?" Dan interrupted. "You *know* you did!"

"Yes, yes, you're right," my friend said, "And I'm sorry. I really am. Please forgive me."

"Look, I know you didn't mean anything by it," Dan said. "And I know you're sincere in your apology. So I forgive you. But it doesn't really end there. I'm going to need some time to work this through." And with that he turned and walked away.

About a week later, my friend's phone rang. When he picked it up, it was Dan on the line. "I just wanted to get back to you about what happened at the retreat day," he said. "I do forgive you. I really do. I mean, I forgave you that day, and I meant it, but . . ."

"I understand," my friend said. "I know just what you were struggling with. I'm glad you didn't put on a plastic smile and tell me, 'Oh it was nothing.' I knew you forgave me that day, but I'm glad you went ahead and really worked things through."

Here is an example that shows how both parties owned their part of the process and there was a genuine healing in their relationship.

Remembering or Blaming?

Back in chapter 7, when I talked about forgiving and forgetting, I made the point that getting clear about "who did what to whom" was crucial to the process of forgiveness. Trying to forget the offenses we have suffered, or to pretend they never happened, is a dead end. We need to *remember* and *accept* the painful things that have been done to us.

What is the difference between this and "blaming"?

"Blaming" is shifting onto others the responsibility that should be ours, or using the fact of others' guilt to *excuse* ourselves from having to *respond* in healthy ways to what was done to us.

Actually, what happens early in the process of forgiveness, the "remembering," may feel the same as blaming. The truth is, for a little bit of time, we need to place the blame where it belongs, and that is usually on someone else. When we are dealing with wounds and injuries that go back to childhood, our tendency to place the blame for what happened on ourselves needs to be changed. If we are going to work through the process of forgiving properly, we need to balance out that tendency by lifting the false blame from ourselves and placing it where the blame really belongs. We need to clearly see that it was not our fault, that we really were victims of someone else.

Blaming can be seductive. If we are not careful, we can reverse the pendulum and become a "blamer." That is why it is essential that we try not to work through this forgiving process alone; we all need the wise counsel of someone we trust. We need to blame at this stage so that we can get an accurate picture of what happened, so that our forgiveness can be solidly grounded in reality. When that happens, we let go of the blame and take responsibility for our own recovery.

Rhonda described herself as a "flaming codependent." Codependency points to destructive lifestyles and emotional patterns that develop from prolonged exposure to an oppressive way of life, usually from living in a close relationship with someone who is "dependent" on alcohol or drugs, or who is in some other way severely dysfunctional. As the sick person's life becomes unmanageable because of his or her dependency, the codependent person's life also becomes unmanageable as a result of trying to cope with them.[3]

When Rhonda's husband began to drink heavily, she moved into a classic codependent stance toward him. She became what is called a *caretaker/enabler*. She cast herself in a role that enabled her husband to avoid facing the consequences of his alcoholism, thus making it easier for him to continue to operate as an alcoholic. If he had a hangover and felt too bad to go to work, she called in and made excuses for him. She figured out ways to hide his drinking from the children. She made life easier for him, thinking she was doing the most loving and helpful thing.

He did not seem to care or even notice all the things she did for him. In fact, he became increasingly abusive toward her as time went on—even insisting that his drinking problem was her fault. "If you were a better cook," he'd shout, "I wouldn't drink so much." Or, "You're such a stupid woman, drinking is the only way I can stand to live with you!" The tragic part is that Rhonda, in spite of herself, believed him. For 14 years she lived under these conditions, convinced that his drinking really *was* her fault—that she *deserved* the treatment he gave her and was not entitled to a better life. Her husband had learned to play the blame game, and she was the perennial loser.

One of the steps Rhonda had to go through to get free from her codependency was to assert and accept that she was *not* the cause of her husband's problems. She was *not* stupid, and her cooking skills (or lack thereof) had nothing whatsoever to do with her husband's drinking. He did not drink because of anything she did or did not do. He drank because he was an alcoholic. The fact was that he was a sick and abusive man who had in fact done her great harm.

Rhonda needed to release herself from false blame and accept the reality of her situation. Not that she turned around and played the blame game herself, laying all her difficulties at her husband's doorstep and absolving herself from all responsibility. Rhonda still had much to learn about responding well to the things that had happened to her, and about living a healthy and fruitful life in her own right. The goal was not to *shift* blame but to *do away with* blame; not to make her husband the villain but to acknowledge and accept what he had done *so that she could forgive him.*

Rhonda's situation was actually rather mild as codependents go. Perhaps the core problem of codependency is this willingness to take all blame upon ourselves for problems that are simply not of our making. People can be beaten, raped, humiliated, half-starved, verbally abused—victimized in any of a dozen ways—and all the while think, *This is my fault. I did something wrong. I made him lose his temper. If I had just been quieter, or if I had responded quicker when he called me, or if I had only sensed his mood when he came in, this wouldn't have happened.*

It is absolutely crucial that such people be able to see that it is *not* their fault, that *someone else* is causing their pain. This is the indispensable first step in being able to forgive that person, which is the only path to freedom, health and sanity.

KEY POINTS TO REMEMBER

1. Placing blame correctly is a healthy part of forgiving.

2. We often need another person's perspective to properly place blame.

3. But blaming can all too easily lead us down the path of bitterness.

4. We can be seduced by the "joy" of bitterness.

5. Continuing to blame leads to a perpetual "pity party."

Notes

1. Leonard Goldenson, "Beating the Odds," *USA Today,* February 27, 1991.

2. Harriet Lerner, *The Dance of Anger* (New York: Harper & Row, 1985), p. 56.

3. For a more complete discussion of codependency, see Robert Hemfelt, M.D., Frank Minirth, M.D. and Paul Meier, M.D., *Love Is a Choice* (Nashville, TN: Thomas Nelson Publishers, 1989).

Confrontation and / or Reconciliation

Sometimes, going to those who have harmed you and clearing the air is helpful. But before you confront, you must carefully discern your motives and assess your expectations. You must also understand that you can, and should, forgive others even if you cannot be reconciled to them.

As a child, Mel remembered two things about his father. First, he remembered that his father was distant—almost silent around him. When he did speak, it was only to complain that Mel had done something wrong. Second, Mel remembered that his father drank heavily. Sometimes when he drank, he would laugh and tell funny stories. Other times he became abusive and hit Mel. Mel never knew which to expect.

Years later, after he had grown up and left home, Mel felt he needed to be free from the harsh memories of life with his father. After an intense struggle, he was able to work his way through the process of forgiveness and release his father from the emotional IOU he had held against him. It was a great day when Mel could finally say, "I've forgiven him."

He then decided to take what seemed like the next logical step: to reconcile with his father. Knowing that he had released himself from the grip of his past was wonderful, but Mel wanted to go further. He wanted to patch things up with his dad and re-store their relationship. Although he now lived almost a thousand miles away from his father, he made a special trip just to spend time with him. "Dad," he said, "could we talk?"

Without saying a word, Mel's father sat down in his favorite chair. Mel pulled up another chair and sat down facing his dad. For nearly 30 minutes, Mel told his dad about the pent-up anger and hurt he had grown up with. He never accused, and carefully avoided saying anything condemnatory about his father's actions. He spoke only of himself, reporting simply and objectively what he had experienced, and how he now wanted to make things right.

At the end he leaned forward and took his father's hand. "Dad," he said, "I've put aside all my anger and hurt. I hope you'll forgive me for the many ways I've failed you. I've always wanted to be a good son, to make you proud of me. That's what I want now—just for us to be a real father and son."

Mel's father had listened the entire time without saying a word or expressing any emotion. Now, as Mel finished, his father pulled himself up from his chair, looked down at Mel, nodded his head slightly, and said, "Well . . ." Then he turned, walked down the hall to his bedroom and quietly closed the door. He did not come out that night or even the next day before Mel left.

Several months later, Mel's father suffered a stroke. He died two hours before Mel reached him.

In reviewing his attempt at reconciliation, Mel spoke of his confusion. When he left his father's house that day, Mel still had no idea how his father felt about what he had said, about what had happened between them, about him—about anything. His dad never gave him the slightest response.

"Why did he act like that?" Mel said. "What did I do wrong?"

"Let's try a different question," I suggested. "What did you *ex-pect* to happen when you talked to him?"

"Expect?" Mel said. He shrugged his shoulders. "I don't know what I expected. Nothing, I guess."

"Really?" I replied. "If you didn't have any expectations, then how could you have been disappointed?"

Mel pondered that for a moment, then began to speak. The words tumbled out. He had hoped for an apology. He had hoped for at least some attempt on his father's part to respond. He had hoped his father would say, "I love you," or at least, "I forgive you." Most of all, perhaps, he had hoped his father would say, "Please forgive me."

"And now he's gone," Mel said with great sadness. He had *forgiven* his father. But he had not been able to *reconcile* with him. It was one of those sad facts of life that so many of us must live with. Mel struggled for a long time over what he considered to be his own failure. Surely he could have made the reconciliation happen if he had just said the right things or said them the right way, or . . .

"The only failure," I finally told Mel, "is that you lumped together two things that are really separate. Forgiveness and reconciliation are not the same thing."

Two Distinct Processes

Forgiveness and reconciliation are not the same thing. It is vitally important that we grasp that distinction. Forgiveness is unilateral. It is something we can do all by ourselves, something we can "make happen" by our own decision. Reconciliation, however, requires the participation of another person. We cannot "make it happen," no matter how hard we try.

Forgiveness and reconciliation are two separate and distinct processes. We *can* have forgiveness without reconciliation. Working through the process of forgiveness is essential to our personal wellbeing and should always be pursued. Reconciliation is immensely valuable to us and should be pursued whenever possible—but it isn't always possible, for reconciliation requires that the other person be active in the healing process.

Mel was stuck on this point. He did not consider his forgiveness of his father to be complete because he and his father had not reconciled. They had not established a relationship of mutual love, or at least mutual respect. He was confusing the two processes of forgiveness and reconciliation.

I pointed out to Mel that as long as he continued to hold this view, his father could continue to hold him hostage, even in his grave. What Mel needed to see was that forgiveness and reconciliation were separate things—that he *had* forgiven his father, fully and completely, even though they had not reconciled.

Mel's situation is not unusual. I frequently find myself listening to people describe their inner struggle to forgive someone—especially someone close to them, and then tell of their frustration over the way their relationship is now continuing. "Now what?" they ask. "Now that I've forgiven him (or her), why can't we get along?" In effect, they are assuming that the other person, by refusing to be reconciled, can "undo" their forgiveness. But that is not the way it works.

"How you relate to them is a different matter," I usually say. "We can address that later, if you like. For now, I just want you to see that you really have forgiven them. You have done what you needed to do, what you *could* do. You have canceled the debt and freed yourself from the obstacles that held you back from inner peace. I know you're not reconciled with them. But you *have* forgiven them. Nothing can change that."

"But I still can't even *talk* to them," one woman, named Jill, objected. Her parents and two sisters had turned against her years ago, when she had gotten heavily involved in drugs. Since then, Jill had changed. She stopped taking drugs, and finished school. Now she held a responsible job in an advertising firm and had been married for three years. "I mean, they won't *let* me talk to them," she continued. "When I call, they hang up as soon as they recognize my voice. All my letters come back marked, 'Return to Sender.' I don't know what to do."

"Have you forgiven them?" I asked her.

"Well, yes, but . . ."

"Then you've done all *you* can do," I said. "Forgiving is *your* job. It's under *your* control. But reconciling? For that you need their cooperation, which doesn't seem likely. There's nothing you can do about that, as far as I can see. But that doesn't mean you haven't forgiven them. You have!"

Jill understood. She continues to hope—as do I—that one day her family will relent and the door to reconciliation will open up. In the meantime, she can only continue to work through the process of forgiveness whenever bitterness or resentment rise up, and grieve over a family that isn't there, at least not for her.

Jewish Teachings on Forgiveness

We often combine forgiveness and reconciliation into one process. Why do we do that? I think it is the influence of Jewish teachings on forgiveness. Several years ago, I was doing a weekend workshop on forgiveness at a church in central Michigan. On Saturday afternoon, a reporter from the local newspaper interviewed us on what we were teaching. She told us she was also going to interview a local professor who was doing research on the physical reactions to forgiveness. She promised to send us a copy of the article.

About a month later, we got the article. She had done a full page for the front of the local section of the Sunday paper. I read it, of course, and was pleased that she clearly understood what we were teaching, and that the professor had been in agreement with what we had said. But she had added a third interview with a local Jewish rabbi. What he said was quite different from what we had said, and it reflected what rabbis have taught in their schools for several thousand years.

Here's basically where we differed. He said that you only have to forgive when someone repents. If the person doesn't repent, you don't have to forgive. He said there are some things that cannot be forgiven, such as murder. The reason being that only the person murdered has the right to forgive, and since he or she is dead, there can be no forgiveness.

And then he added that one only needs to forgive three times. If you hurt me once, twice or three times, I am required to forgive you. But if you hurt me the same way a fourth time, I no longer need to forgive you, and I am the righteous one for not forgiving.

I understood these things. In my other book on forgiveness, *Forgiving the Unforgivable,* I quoted from the Mishnah a rabbi who taught that you only had to forgive three times; but if it was your rabbi or pastor, you needed to forgive him a thousand times.

What is interesting is that there is really nothing in the Old Testament about forgiving each other. Yes, there are some illustrations in some of the accounts, like where Joseph forgives his brothers (see Gen. 50:15-21). But the focus of the Old Testament is how we get God's forgiveness.

Obviously, Israel needed help in understanding how to forgive someone who had hurt them, so the rabbis had to pull together their own teachings, and this covered the teachings over several thousand years. So what this rabbi was saying in the newspaper article was the same thing that Jesus was taught in His Hebrew school, and what Peter was taught in his Hebrew school. You only needed to forgive three times.

That helps us understand better the conversation between Peter and Jesus in Matthew 18. Jesus' teaching on forgiveness here was very radical, especially in the context of what He had been taught. He said in several places that we must forgive (see Matt. 6:14; 18:33-35; Luke 17:3-4). But then He said something that was totally new to everyone, including the disciples. Peter was blown away by it, so he came to Jesus with some new insight. He asked Jesus, "Lord, how often should I forgive someone who sins against me? Seven times?" Jesus' answer went beyond belief when He said, "No, not seven times . . . but seventy times seven!" (Matt. 18:21-22). That's 490 times, which means there is no limit to our forgiveness.

In several places, Jesus reinforced His demand that we forgive when He said that if someone comes to you in repentance, you must forgive. He uses the "seven times" in Luke 17:4 when He said, "Even if that person wrongs you seven times a day and each time turns again and asks forgiveness, you must forgive."

Paul expanded on this radical teaching when he said several times that we are to forgive as we have been forgiven (see Eph. 4:32) and remember that the Lord has forgiven us, so we must forgive others (see Col. 3:13).

This all makes forgiveness not an option but an act of obedience. I cannot be dependent on someone else's involvement when

I forgive. If I am to be obedient, I have no choice: I must forgive. But reconciliation is another process, and it is a two-way process.

A Two-Way Street

Reconciliation is a two-way street. It requires two people who are at least somewhat in sync with each other. It can occur only when both parties to a relationship want it to happen; when both have accepted their own responsibility for what went wrong, have sorted out their emotions and worked through the processes of both repentance and forgiveness. You work through your side of it and ask for my forgiveness; I work through my side of it and ask for your forgiveness. Then we can be reconciled.

Some of the confusion between reconciliation and forgiveness comes from a too quick reading of Matthew 5:23-24, where Jesus said, "If you are presenting a sacrifice at the altar in the Temple and you suddenly remember that someone has something against you, leave your sacrifice there at the altar. Go and be reconciled to that person. Then come and offer your sacrifice to God." We sometimes miss the "someone has something against you." This is instruction to the offending person, not the forgiving person.

In the well-known story of the prodigal son, a young man takes his inheritance, leaves his family and wastes all his money in a faraway city. Broke and hungry, he makes the difficult decision to come back home and seek reconciliation with his family. In heartrending terms, he begs his father to take him back: "Father, I have sinned against both heaven and you, and I am no longer worthy of being called your son. Please take me on as a hired servant" (Luke 15:18-19).

Clearly, the young man has had a change of heart. Whatever grievances he once held against his father (those things that prompted him to run away in the first place) have clearly been dealt with. He canceled whatever "debt" he once held against his father and came to him repentant, seeking to be reconciled.

How does the father respond? He, too, appears to have released his son from whatever IOUs he may have held against him.

"And while he was still a long way off, his father saw him coming. Filled with love and compassion, he ran to his son, embraced him, and kissed him" (Luke 15:20). What a classic picture of repentance, forgiveness and reconciliation! But then we meet a third character—the older brother:

> Meanwhile, the older son was in the fields working. When he returned home, he heard music and dancing in the house, and he asked one of the servants what was going on. "Your brother is back," he was told, "and your father has killed the fattened calf. We are celebrating because of his safe return." The older brother was angry and wouldn't go in. His father came out and begged him, but he replied, "All these years I've slaved for you and never once refused to do a single thing you told me to. And in all that time you never gave me even one young goat for a feast with my friends. Yet when this son of yours comes back, after squandering your money on prostitutes, you celebrate by killing the fattened calf!" (Luke 15:25-30).

The older brother, in contrast to his father, offers us a picture of reconciliation spurned. Clearly, he still bears great resentment toward his younger brother for his reckless behavior. He also seems to be bitter toward his father for welcoming the younger brother back. As the story unfolds, we see the father attempting to be reconciled to his eldest son, trying to explain his actions in forgiving the younger brother. As far as we know, the older brother was unwilling to be reconciled to either his brother or his father.

*Rifts between me and my relatives or former
friends can often be healed by swallowing my pride
and making the first overtures toward reconciliation.
Even if only a little of the blame was mine, the
generous gesture will benefit me.*

AL-ANON FAMILY GROUP HEAD, INC.,
ONE DAY AT A TIME IN AL-ANON[1]

Reconciliation is a two-way street; in the story of the father and the older and younger brothers, forgiveness flowed in only one direction, and reconciliation was not possible. The father and the younger brother were free from the prison of their bitterness and resentment; but the older brother was still held bound by his.

A Form of Love

Forgiveness is ultimately a form of love, a love that accepts others as they are. It meets others with a compassion that springs from an awareness of our own weaknesses, faults and destructive tendencies.

As we have seen, the one who knows that he has offended another must apologize and work through the process of repentance. This must never be allowed to become a form of "buying back" the relationship. Such a person may struggle with the desire to make some impossible act of restitution, or to be punished in some unhealthy way—as though by doing so he or she could *earn* forgiveness. It may be right to make restitution for a wrong done, but restitution can never earn forgiveness. It is freely offered as an act of love and freely accepted as an act of humility.

We cannot pay for what is freely given to us. The beauty of both forgiveness and reconciliation is that they are free actions that come from the heart. When we have wronged someone, and that person has forgiven us and has opened the door of reconciliation to us, the only thing we can do is accept it. This can be difficult indeed. Accepting unconditional love may make us more keenly aware of our own failures or the wrongness of our own actions. I suspect it was this prospect that rendered Mel's father incapable of accepting his son's offer of reconciliation. As we saw in that case, this refusal to accept forgiveness and love makes reconciliation impossible. Reconciliation is based on mutual acceptance.

Reconciliation requires not only mutual forgiveness but also mutual acceptance. Acceptance is based on:

- Both parties being able to accept themselves
- Both being willing to admit their failures
- Both desiring healing for the ruptured relationship
- Both being prepared to surrender their demand for self-justification
- Both being prepared to set aside their desire to punish the other
- Both acknowledging that it is not easy for people to receive unconditional, forgiving love

Reconciliation Without Forgiveness

I have pointed out that it is possible to forgive without reconciling. It is also possible to reconcile without truly forgiving. This happens in these situations:

- When we "overlook" the pain caused by someone's actions
- When we deny that we've been hurt
- When we excuse inexcusable behavior
- When we fear that we'll lose the relationship if we speak up

"I could be reconciled to my wife," one man said to me. "It's easy. I've done it dozens of times. All I have to do is admit that I've been the monster she says I am, and that all the hurtful things she says are true. And just like that, we're reconciled."

"And you end up despising yourself," I offered. With pain too deep for words, he nodded slowly. If only she would enter the process with him.

Let's take another example. Say that you've wounded me in some way. It cuts deeply. I go to you and tell you how hurt I am. But immediately I add, "I know you didn't mean it the way I took it. If I could only get over my sensitivity about things like that." I end up apologizing to *you* for your hurting me!

How absurd! Yet many of us do it all the time! We have been taught that we must be willing to do *anything* to bring about peace—even deny the truth and inflict wounds on ourselves. We end up struggling to find some way to persuade the other person (and ourselves) that we caused the rupture in the first place.

It's easy to be "reconciled" under that approach! But what has happened isn't really reconciliation at all. Reconciliation has to proceed from forgiveness. The work of forgiveness has to take place in both parties before they can make any step toward one another. Earlier, I spoke of "superficial forgiveness." Now you can see that superficial forgiveness leads only to artificial reconciliation.

Letting Bygones Be Bygones

I want to emphasize that I believe in the importance of reconciliation whenever it is possible and mutually beneficial, especially in a marriage. But reconciliation doesn't happen in every instance, no matter how much one party may want it.

For one thing, as we have seen, reconciliation requires that both parties be willing participants. That may not happen. You may go to the other person having fully forgiven them, and with the genuine desire to be reconciled, only to have them reject your efforts. We have seen several examples of this dynamic already.

Sometimes, efforts at reconciliation need to be sought with caution. In cases of physical, sexual or other kinds of abuse, it may not be safe to reconcile with the people who have wronged us. Such people may still be dangerous to us, and it may be better to keep our distance from them. Or they may be in such a fragile condition that confronting them with the past might devastate them. There *are* times when it is wisest to let bygones be bygones, at least as far as confrontation and reconciliation are concerned. However, it is *never* advisable to bypass the process of forgiveness.

When the Other Person Is No Longer Living

Sometimes, of course, confrontation and reconciliation are not possible because the other person is no longer living. The most common example is when we want to be reconciled to a parent who has died. There may, however, be ways to apply the dynamics of confrontation even in such instances.

- Glen went to his father's grave. There he poured out his heart about the things that had happened between them and how Glen wished things could have been. "I don't know if he could hear me," Glen said. "I guess it doesn't really matter. I was able to say the things I needed to say."

- Maria took down a large framed portrait of her father from the wall and spoke to it. "I remember gazing intently at every feature of his face," she said, "like I was trying to look into his soul." She did this a number of times over a period of months. Finally, she was able to say, "Dad, I forgive you."

- Art went back to his childhood home, a rustic cottage in the woods. He explained to the current owners that he had lived there as a boy and wanted to see the place again. They gave him permission to stroll through the woods. As he walked, he talked to his long-dead parents.

- Felicia wrote a lengthy obituary about her parents. While she recalled the bad treatment she had received, she was also able to reflect on happy memories. That in itself was healing; in her days of pain, she had been able to remember nothing but the hurtful memories.

- Andrea asked a married couple in her church, a couple she knew well and respected deeply, to "sit in" as surrogate parents. Then she talked through with them some of what she had experienced from her real parents.

Does there seem to be an element of make-believe in these techniques? I am not contending that these exercises are the same as actual, concrete, face-to-face confrontation and reconciliation.

But they *do* bring to bear some of the same dynamics in a way that helps advance the process of forgiveness.

Besides, in many cases, what people really need to deal with is not so much their literal flesh-and-blood present-day parents as much as the *memory picture* of their parents *as they once were*. Most of us carry around within us such a memory picture of those who hurt us. It may be that those people have changed in the intervening years—that those who hurt us, in a sense, no longer exist. Our main need, in such a case, may not be to confront our parents *as they are now*, but to confront them *as they were then*. The kinds of exercises described above can be excellent tools for doing that.

Some Cautions about Confrontation

Some years ago, confronting one's parents was all the rage. We had friends whose son was in counseling. When they went to visit, the son asked if they would go with him to his counselor. They agreed.

However, it was all a set-up. For the whole session, the son confronted the parents for all the terrible things they had done to him while growing up. When the session was over, our friends returned to their son's home, packed their things and went home. The parents and the son never spoke again—the parents' hurt was too deep, and the son wasn't satisfied. When the mother died, the father and the son talked. But the mother never had the opportunity to experience healing in that relationship. How sad! And how unnecessary. The goal is never to confront. It is always to heal.

When confrontations and other efforts at reconciliation are thoughtfully planned, and a person's attitudes and expectations are properly adjusted, such efforts can be a great help to the healing process. But they need to be carefully planned and can never be a place to simply dump all of our pain on the other person.

Back in chapter 1, we met Lydia, who had been molested by her stepfather with the full knowledge of her mother. She and her therapist decided it would be important for her to confront her parents with the truth about what had happened and how it had affected her.

Lydia spent several days writing out what she wanted to say and going over it with her therapist. She rehearsed it in her support group. Other members of the group even played the parts of her parents, giving Lydia a chance to practice handling different kinds of responses. When the day came, Lydia handled her part perfectly. She didn't get into blaming. She didn't lose control and get angry. She just told her parents, calmly and objectively, what she wanted them to know.

Neither parent responded. They just sat there and denied everything Lydia had said. They were quite pleasant and polite about it, but completely unyielding in their denial. When Lydia's therapist tried to talk to them about how they were responding, they shut that out as well.

But Lydia was prepared. She had gone into the session knowing that her parents might deny everything. When it was over, she told the others in her group that she felt relieved, as if a tremendous weight had been lifted from her shoulders. "It was like I set the truth on the table and they were free to do whatever they wanted with it," she said. "If they wanted to ignore it, that was their business. But at least I wasn't lugging it around by myself anymore."

Lydia's story demonstrates how we can be at peace even when reconciliation isn't possible. Lydia was at peace. She felt the need to test and see if reconciliation might be possible. When it turned out not to be, she wasn't thrown off. She knew that forgiveness was separate from reconciliation. And she knew that whether or not she ever reconciled with her parents, she *had* forgiven them. She had done everything that was in her power to do. She was released from the burden of the past.

Those of us who have worked through the process of forgiveness have the deep satisfaction of knowing that we can survive injury—and not only survive, but flourish. No matter how deep the wound, no matter how bitter the pain, once we forgive, we are no longer victims or mere survivors. We are victors! We have fought through to the ultimate triumph. We have learned to love.

KEY POINTS TO REMEMBER

1. Confrontation never resolves family issues of the past.

2. Reconciliation requires repentance on the part of the offender.

3. Reconciliation is separate from forgiving and best follows after the forgiving.

4. Jesus' teachings on forgiveness, as well as the apostle Paul's teachings, are radical.

5. Forgiveness is an act of obedience on our part; reconciliation is an option.

6. Forgiveness is a form of love.

7. We can do the work of forgiving even if the other person is no longer living.

Note

1. Al-Anon Family Group Head, Inc., *One Day at a Time in Al-Anon* (New York: Al-Anon Family Group Headquarters, Inc., 1987), p. 175.

11

Forgiving My Parents, Forgiving Myself

You and your parents may have been "partners in crime" in perpetuating harmful family dynamics. You need to accept responsibility for the ways you may have contributed to your own pain—and then learn to forgive yourself and go on.

"I don't think I've ever met anyone who hated his parents," a colleague once said to me, "who didn't also hate himself."

I think he was right. Our sense of self is derived so strongly from our parents that what we think about them is inevitably going to shape what we think about ourselves. If we hate our parents, it is likely that we will struggle with some degree of self-hatred. If we love our parents, it is likely that we will feel better about ourselves.

It stands to reason that if we find ourselves needing to *forgive* our parents—and as adult children of dysfunctional families, we do almost by definition—we will also find that we need to forgive ourselves.

"Honor Thy Father and Mother . . ."

All of us recognize that there is no such thing as a perfect parent. All of us are descended from imperfect parents and grew up in imperfect families. However, to acknowledge this as an intellectual proposition is one thing; but to actually admit that our parents have failed us is, for some of us, a very hard thing to do.

It may even seem like a *wrong* thing to do. Doesn't the Bible teach that we are supposed to honor our father and mother (see Exod. 20:12)? Indeed we are. But what does it mean to *honor* our parents? Does it mean we should never acknowledge their weaknesses, limitations and mistakes? Does it mean we should never acknowledge the pain they may have caused us? I don't think so.

The original Hebrew word used in the Exodus passage literally means "assign weight to." It is as though someone told us something and we replied, "I want to carefully *weigh* what you've said." If we consider their words and decide they are important, we are, in a sense "assigning weight" to them. Thus, to "honor" our parents means to assign weight—value, importance, significance—to them.

When that original Hebrew word was translated into Greek for the New Testament, the Greek word had to do with "giving glory to" the thing being honored. Both the Greek and the Hebrew carried the sense of honoring people *because of the position they held,* not necessarily because of intrinsic value. One way to understand this is to imagine that you are in a banquet hall. Partway through the banquet, your city mayor walks in. Now let's suppose that you are not particularly fond of this mayor. You didn't vote for him in the last election, and you think he has made some bad decisions. Even so, when he walks into the room, you stand up along with everyone else to greet him.

Why? Because he is the mayor, and honoring him is the appropriate thing to do. You assign a certain value, or "weight," to him because of the position he holds. This does not mean you now have to start liking him or even respecting him as a person. It does not mean you have to start pretending that you agree with everything he has done as mayor. The honor is accorded to the position he holds, not so much to the individual.

In the same way, we can honor our parents—accord them an appropriate degree of weight—because of the position they hold in our lives as our parents. Similar to my example with the mayor, the fact that we honor our parents does not mean we have to pretend that they have never done anything wrong or hurtful to us.

It is *healthy*, not dishonoring, to acknowledge that our parents failed us, hurt us or damaged us in some way—especially if we are doing so *for the sake of forgiving them*. We do neither our parents nor ourselves any honor by denying reality, eliminating the possibility of forgiveness, and locking ourselves into dysfunctional patterns of thinking and acting. Health and wholeness require that we be honest with ourselves.

Denying the Past

There are a number of common ways in which we try to protect ourselves from truth about our past.

Denying Our Past

1. We deny that any injury ever occurred.
2. We make excuses for our parents.
3. We put the blame on ourselves.
4. We grant superficial forgiveness.
5. We attack those who suggest that we need to forgive.

1. We Deny that Any Injury Ever Occurred

I often talk to people who are unable to remember anything about their early years. In many cases, this is a strong indication of childhood trauma. Without consciously realizing it, we substitute an idealized picture for the unpleasant reality.

When we do this, we will have a strong instinct to protect our parents (and often, other authority figures as well). We may even believe it is wrong to be angry with them or to have any feelings toward them other than total love and devotion.

Some people honestly believe that if they are angry with their parents, something bad will happen to them. A woman named

Shirley said to me, "I don't expect to live to old age." When I
asked her why, she pointed to the biblical commandment about
honoring parents: "If you honor your father and mother, things
will go well for you, and you will have a long life on the earth"
(Eph. 6:3).

"I gave my parents a lot of trouble," she said, "so I guess I'll
have to pay the consequences." I had to point out to her that this
is an exhortation given to an entire people and has to do with so-
cietal welfare—not with punishment visited upon individuals.

2. We Make Excuses for Our Parents

We say things like, "Well, yes, my dad beat me a lot. But my folks
were having financial troubles at the time." Or, "My parents
never showed me affection—I don't remember them ever even
hugging me. But they were doing the best they could under the
circumstances." Or, "It wasn't as bad as what some of my friends
experienced."

Others go back a generation and look at how their parents
were raised, and use that as a way of excusing their behavior to
them while they were growing up. I often suggest to people like
this that their parents also apparently did nothing to break the
pattern, as they were now attempting to do by being in counseling.

3. We Put the Blame on Ourselves

"I had a lot of bad times growing up. I was a little terror to raise. I
gave my parents a bad time most of the time. So I deserved everything I got. If I had been more thoughtful (or more helpful, or
more obedient or whatever), my parents wouldn't have had to treat
me the way they did."

4. We Grant Superficial Forgiveness

"Whatever they did to me, I forgive them." Or, "Sure, they made
mistakes, just like everybody else. I don't hold anything against
them." Of course, when we do this, we really don't have much of
a relationship with our parents. It's all based on empty words
and actions.

5. We Attack Those Who Suggest that We Need to Forgive
"How could you even think such a thing?" The traumatic memories of growing up in a dysfunctional family are not easy to live with. Before forgiveness can happen, however, we need to acknowledge and accept as much of the pain as we can. We need to feel the hurt, just as we felt it in childhood, in order to let it go. When we have progressed to the place where we can see our parents objectively, we can begin the process of forgiving. Along the way, we will also see more clearly the ways *we* have failed. Then we must also begin the process of forgiving ourselves.

Shedding Illusions

Gaining freedom from the effects of growing up in an unhealthy, dysfunctional family is a learning process. We learn to accept ourselves, even with our limitations and vulnerabilities. We learn that life in this world entails the possibility of injury for all of us.

We also learn that some of our long-protected illusions about ourselves and others must change. Childhood expectations and idealizations of the way people should behave may wind up influencing us long into adulthood, with harmful results.

For example, it is a common childhood expectation that all families are happy: Mom cheerfully takes care of the kids' every need; dad goes off to work each morning with a smile on his face and returns each night for dinner; the family schedules all kinds of fun outings for the weekends; everyone is happy and fulfilled all the time. That picture of "normal" family life is reinforced in dozens of ways: in the storybooks we read in school, in the shows we watched on television, and so on.

As we grow older, we recognize that this rosy picture is an idealization, not the norm. We recognize that few, if any, families really look or act this way. We recognize that our own family does not look or act this way.

Or do we? In some cases, it is more accurate to say that part of us recognizes and accepts the unreality of this picture. But another part of us clings to it desperately, still believing it to be true, and ever more conscious of the ways in which our own situation falls short.

In working through the process of forgiveness, we need to figure out how our own expectations may have set the stage for our being hurt. Part of maturity is accepting responsibility for our own outlook on life and relationships. If others have hurt us by failing to live up to our expectations, then one of the things we need to do is to examine whether those expectations may have been inappropriate and unrealistic.

Once they are dead, we want our parents to be sheer light, with no darkness at all; and we feel a little foul if we allow shadows to darken our memory. We don't want them to need forgiving; because if we forgive them, we must have found fault with them first, maybe even hated them.

LEWIS B. SMEDES, *FORGIVE AND FORGET:*
HEALING THE HURTS WE DON'T DESERVE[1]

If so, forgiveness for us will need to involve repentance (a fundamental change of our own minds and hearts about what we should rightly expect from others) as well as our working through our pain. The pain of unmet expectations is still very real and still needs to be dealt with, even if those expectations *were* unrealistic.

Stephen's father had physically abused him. His younger brother, the family favorite, was never punished and had always been allowed to do as he pleased. Stephen, understandably, needed to work through his feelings of anger toward his father. But he also found himself struggling with self-hatred and resentful feelings toward his brother, even though he knew it was not his brother's fault that he had been the favorite or that Stephen had been the whipping boy. Yet Stephen grew up believing that somehow he *deserved* punishment, while his brother deserved to be treated well.

Stephen was talking through his feelings with his pastor. At one point he cried out, "My father loved my brother, and he hated me!"

His pastor asked in return, "Do you think you deserved your mistreatment?"

"That's how I feel," Stephen answered. He went on to catalog a number of ways in which he had let his father down.

"And you can forgive your father, but you can't forgive yourself because of your failures. Is that it?" the pastor questioned.

"I just keep thinking I'm not *worth* forgiving," Stephen replied. "I know things about myself that other people don't know."

The pastor sat quietly for a moment, thinking. Then he said, "Let's try something. I want you to imagine that you're another person, a different person, sitting in that chair over there, talking to 'Stephen.' Do you understand?"

"Yes."

"Now then, let's say 'Stephen' has offended you. Will you decide to forgive him?"

"Well . . . sure. Of course."

"Even if he doesn't ask you to forgive him?"

Stephen nodded.

"Why?" the pastor asked.

Stephen thought for a moment. "Whether he asks or not isn't the issue. The issue is whether or not I'm willing to forgive."

"Exactly!" the pastor exclaimed. "Now, think about it for a minute. You say you're willing to be compassionate and forgiving toward 'Stephen' for hurting you. But the fact of the matter is, 'Stephen' is *you*. You have been offended by *yourself*. Now you need to be willing to *forgive* yourself. Do you understand?"

Stephen took a long time to think before he responded. "I never thought of it that way," he finally said. "But I see what you mean. Forgiving myself isn't really any different than forgiving anyone else. Even if I've done things wrong, even if I've caused myself a great deal of pain, I can still forgive myself. I don't need to go around blaming myself, being angry at myself, all the time. Right?"

Right!

How unhappy is he who cannot forgive himself.
PUBLILIUS SYRUS

The Most Difficult Person to Forgive: Myself

Freedom from the wounds of the past begins when we acknowledge to ourselves that others are in some way responsible for the hurt we have experienced. But we cannot stop there. We also need to face and forgive *ourselves,* for there are certainly things we have done that we regret.

For many of us, the most difficult person to forgive is self. As hard as forgiveness is to learn, most of us have a much easier time learning to forgive others than we do learning to forgive ourselves. We are capable of feeling far more compassion toward others than toward ourselves.

If we have been raised in an unhealthy, dysfunctional home that encouraged blaming ourselves for anything bad that happened, it will be especially difficult to forgive ourselves. How many of us harbor such thoughts as the following deep inside us?

"Somehow I allowed all this to happen."

"I deserve this pain."

"It's all my fault."

"I could have stopped it from happening, but I didn't."

It is bad enough when self-blaming thoughts like these are untrue—when we are *not* really to blame but saddle ourselves with guilt anyway. But what about when they *are* true? What about when we *have* done wrong, when we *have* helped bring about our own suffering—and we know it?

We need to learn to accept ourselves, with all of our limitations, failings and vulnerabilities, just as we learn to accept others. Indeed, we need to learn how to work through the process of forgiveness with ourselves, just as we have learned to do it toward others.

Let's review briefly the process of forgiveness as outlined in chapter 6—but this time, instead of looking at it in terms of forgiving someone else, look at it in terms of forgiving yourself.

1. Recognize the Injury
You need to answer the same kinds of questions you answered before. What happened? What role did I play in it? What did I do

> **Forgiving Myself**
>   1. Recognize the injury.
>   2. Identify the emotions involved.
>   3. Express the feelings.
>   4. Set boundaries to protect yourself.
>   5. Cancel the debt.

that was mistaken or wrong? I talked before about making up a list of "sins done to me." Here you are making a list of "sins done to me *by* me."

Again, the aim is not to heap scorn on yourself, or to blame yourself—you have done enough of that already—the aim is simply to get clear on what happened so that you can deal with it cleanly.

In taking this step, you need to be especially careful to take responsibility only for those things that *are* your responsibility. Adult children of dysfunctional families typically feel that everything that goes wrong in life is somehow their fault. But you can rightfully accept responsibility only for what you actually did. You cannot accept responsibility for what you could not have done, could not foresee or could not have known about. You are responsible only for those things that are under your control, not for the entire world.

> *That which we can excuse we need not forgive; only*
> *that which we cannot excuse is in need of forgiveness.*
> DAN HAMILTON, *FORGIVENESS*[2]

In other words, you may at times need to *excuse* yourself rather than *forgive* yourself. To excuse yourself is simply to say, "Yes, I made a mistake there. But it wasn't my fault. There's no way I could have known to do it any differently." Or, "Yes, something did indeed go wrong there. But I didn't do it. Just because my parents always blamed me for everything doesn't mean that everything was actually my fault."

Once you have sorted out what actually happened, and what you actually did that was wrong, you are ready to take the next step.

2. Identify the Emotions Involved

As you clarify the ways you have been injured, a familiar set of emotions will rise to the surface. Earlier we identified them as fear, guilt, shame and anger. When you are looking into injuries you have inflicted upon yourself, the predominant emotions will probably be anger and shame. Self-directed anger and shame are often prime causes of depression.

3. Express the Feelings

You need some way to get the poison of these negative emotions out of your system. The same techniques we discussed before will work here:

- Talk it out with a friend.
- Write out what happened and how it felt in a journal.
- "Talk to yourself" about it, much as the pastor encouraged Stephen to do.

4. Set Boundaries to Protect Yourself

Previously we talked about taking steps to protect ourselves from others. Now you must consider protecting yourself from yourself.

Many times your negative feelings about yourself will prompt you to engage in self-destructive behavior:

- You may overeat.
- You may starve yourself and become anorexic or bulimic.
- You may abuse alcohol or drugs (including prescription drugs).
- You may overdo your exercise program, staying at it until you're ready to collapse.
- You may engage in unhealthy, illicit or dangerous sexual behavior.

- You may become antagonistic toward others, hard to live with or work with, in ways that trigger antagonistic responses in people around you. The onset of such destructive behaviors can alert you that there is a need for self-examination and self-forgiveness. In addition, these behaviors *cause* you injury and, as a result, further self-loathing. Thus, dealing with them is doubly important not only because of the direct damage they cause, but also because of the impact they have on your emotional health.

5. Cancel the Debt

You deal with them in precisely the same way—by canceling the debt. Often, it can be helpful to have the act of forgiveness take some concrete, tangible form such as writing out a "bill of particulars" and then marking it "canceled" or burning or burying it.

Why Self-Forgiveness Is So Hard

When I first talked about this process, I said that the forgiveness we show to others comes from the forgiveness God has shown to us; *our forgiveness flows from our forgiven-ness*. Nowhere is this more true than in forgiving ourselves.

No matter how grievously you may have injured yourself, Jesus' death on the cross freed you. The grace of God is *always* sufficient. His forgiveness is *always* adequate. No matter how unloved or worthless you may feel, God loves you. Your feelings about yourself do not change God's love for you. He gave each of us infinite worth and value, by creating us and by sending His Son to die for us. If God Himself is able to forgive us, how can we withhold forgiveness from ourselves?

Because you have been forgiven, your obligation is to forgive those who do wrong to you, without exception—this includes yourself.

I often talk with people about this and ask, "Has God forgiven you?"

They are quick to respond, "Oh, yes, I know He's forgiven me, but I just can't forgive myself."

I then say, "That's interesting. I guess you have higher standards than God for this forgiving thing. It's not a good idea to not forgive what God has forgiven!"

So why do we withhold forgiveness from ourselves? One of the main reasons why we have difficulty with the notion of "forgiving ourselves" is simply that we have never seen forgiveness demonstrated. As with so many things in life, it is a great help to have seen forgiveness modeled by others if we are to understand and practice it ourselves. Adult children from unhealthy, dysfunctional families typically grew up in environments where forgiveness was not modeled. And when it comes to forgiving yourself, you need to not only have a model of forgiving, you also need to really focus in on the reality of God's forgiveness of you.

"No matter how hard I tried," Ralph told me, "nothing I ever did was good enough for my dad. Even when I told him how sorry I was and that I'd try harder next time, do you know what he said to me? He'd say, 'Do it right *this* time.' I never knew what it was like to have a mistake or a weakness *tolerated,* let alone accepted or forgiven."

"In our home, love was a manipulation device," recalls Allison. She came from a home where both parents were alcoholics. "When my mother said, 'I love you,' it only meant that she wanted something. She said it with a smile on her face, but she didn't really mean it. Even when she said something that sounded like she was forgiving me for making a mistake, I couldn't believe her. I knew she was just doing it to try to get something from me."

It's no wonder that people like Ralph and Allison find the notion of forgiveness hard to grasp—whether it is forgiveness of others or, even more, forgiveness of self.

Another reason why we find it hard to forgive ourselves is that we have the mistaken idea that if we withhold forgiveness from ourselves it will protect us from ever doing such a thing again. This is a false idea and may actually help set us up to repeat the offense. Remember, the purpose of forgiving is to find freedom, and the purpose of forgiving yourself is that same sense of freedom.

A third reason can be the fact that we are trying to keep everything we need to forgive ourselves for a secret. James tells us to "confess your sins to each other and pray for each other so that you may be healed" (Jas. 5:16). We really cannot forgive ourselves in isolation, holding the offense as a secret within. We need to have someone we trust who will hear our confession and pray for us. Then God promises the healing we desire.

Self-Forgiveness for Abuse Victims

Those who come from a background of emotional or physical abuse (and especially sexual abuse) often struggle with the belief that something is inherently wrong with them. They think that something about their very being made the bad things happen to them. They *deserved* the wounds they received. They see themselves as unworthy, unlovable and unforgivable.

The fact that they came from a home where secrecy was so prevalent makes them feel even worse about themselves. "Don't talk" is always a cardinal rule in abusive homes. I have talked with women who actually hate their own bodies for causing their fathers (or uncles or brothers) to desire them. "I must have been inviting it somehow or they wouldn't have kept doing it" is a familiar sentiment. They even blame themselves for the fact that no one protected or assisted them.

Often, incest victims experience a certain measure of physical pleasure even amidst the emotional pain of being violated. This only intensifies their shame. If it felt good, doesn't that prove they secretly wanted it to happen? One of the things we work hard to teach incest survivors is that the body can respond to sexual stimuli even without the person's consent. Still, this apparent betrayal by their own bodies can be one of the hardest things for them to forgive—especially when it is compounded by the ingrained belief that if they tell anyone what happened, they will only receive more blame and condemnation.

For all those who have been victims or have suffered the pain of growing up in a dysfunctional family, one of the most important truths of life is summed up in this saying of Jesus: " 'Love the LORD your God with all your heart, all your soul, and all your mind.' This is the first and greatest commandment. A second is equally important: 'Love your neighbor as yourself' " (Matt. 22:37-39).

Most of us are well aware that the Bible commands us to love God and to love our neighbor. But I want you to notice two little words in this passage. Jesus says, "Love your neighbor *as yourself.*"

Many people struggle with the idea that we are supposed to love ourselves. It sounds so selfish. Actually, Jesus does not so much teach that we *should* love ourselves as He *assumes* that we *do* love ourselves. And why not? Are we not created in the very image and likeness of God? Is our welfare not of such importance to God that even the hairs on our heads are all numbered (see Matt. 10:30)? Should we not love the things God loves, including ourselves?

I am not talking here about the kind of self-love that expresses itself in self-glorification, narcissism, despising others, and so on. Rather, I am talking about a self-love that acknowledges our worth and dignity as one of God's sons or daughters and acts accordingly. We have already seen that our duty to love our neighbor includes forgiving them when they do us wrong. Should we not likewise be able to forgive ourselves?

Stopping the Abuse

If you are a man or woman who grew up in a dysfunctional family, and you are trying to break free from the wounds of your past by forgiving your parents and others, recognize that you will also need to work through the process of forgiveness with yourself. As you do, think about these statements:

- If I continue to accept blame, *the abuse is continuing.*
- If I accept guilt for what happened even when I was a help-less child, *the abuse is continuing.*
- If I continue to accept pain, guilt and shame just because that's what I've always done, *the abuse is continuing.*
- If I refuse to be compassionate, loving and forgiving toward myself, *the abuse is continuing.*

Why not put a stop to the abuse—to all of it—right now? Release yourself from the unhealthy burden of guilt you have placed upon yourself, even for such things as your depression, your withdrawal, your self-doubt and your lack of trust. As you work through the process of forgiving yourself, looking back on times when you let yourself down, you might find it helpful to bear in mind this statement:

> *I did the best I could with the maturity, knowledge and wisdom I had.*
> *Now, with more maturity, knowledge and wisdom, I can do better.*

Self-forgiveness is not a matter of assigning blame to someone else and letting yourself off the hook; it is not a license for irresponsibility. It is simply an acknowledgment that you are a human being like everybody else. It can be a celebration of survival and of the fact that you've reached the stage where you are able to give yourself greater respect.

> *Forgiveness is another way of saying, "I'm human.*
> *I make mistakes. I want to be granted that privilege,*
> *and so I grant you that privilege."*
> PHILIP YANCEY, "AN UNNATURAL ACT"[3]

An interesting thing often happens when we work through the process of forgiving ourselves. We find that for the first time we are able to say some important things to ourselves without feeling guilty or ashamed:

- I was, and still am, imperfect.
- I had, and still have, angry feelings.
- I held, and still hold, some unrealistic expectations.
- I have failed, and still fail, to live up to what I know is right.

We can comfortably say these things because we have also said and believed this: "For all these things—and many more besides—

I forgive *myself.* I forgive myself because God has already forgiven me. And with His help, I'm going to become better and better in the future."

KEY POINTS TO REMEMBER:

1. Hating my parents and hating myself go hand in hand.

2. Honoring my parents means "honoring what is honorable"— I do not honor what is not honorable.

3. I must face my past to resolve it.

4. The most difficult person to forgive is myself.

5. Forgiving myself comes out of the context of understanding how much I have been forgiven by God.

6. There is no benefit in not forgiving myself. The opposite is true: I am set free when I forgive myself.

Notes

1. Lewis B. Smedes, *Forgive and Forget: Healing the Hurts We Don't Deserve* (New York: Harper & Row, 1984).

2. Dan Hamilton, *Forgiveness* (Downers Grove, IL: Intervarsity Press, 1980), p. 145.

3. Philip Yancey, "An Unnatural Act," *Christianity Today* (April 8, 1991), p. 39.

Forgiveness and the Twelve Steps

For more than 70 years—and especially during the last 30 years—millions of people have found help for problems relating to dependency and dysfunction through the programs based on the Twelve Steps of Alcoholics Anonymous. While originally written for those addicted to alcohol, the Twelve Steps have been modified for application to a wide range of problems, such as drug addiction, sex addiction, overeating, compulsive gambling, codependency relationships with addicted spouses and—yes, adult children of dysfunctional families.

Although everything in this book is entirely compatible with a Twelve Step approach to recovery, I have not specifically focused on the Twelve Steps. For the many readers who are familiar with this approach to recovery, however, it is worth considering the problems of adult children of dysfunctional families in the light of the Twelve Steps.

The Twelve Steps of Alcoholics Anonymous[1]

1. We admitted we were powerless over alcohol—that our lives had become unmanageable.
2. Came to believe that a power greater than ourselves could restore us to sanity.
3. Made a decision to turn our will and our lives over to the care of God *as we understood him.*
4. Made a searching and fearless moral inventory of ourselves.
5. Admitted to God, to ourselves, and to another human being the exact nature of our wrongs.
6. Were entirely ready to have God remove all these defects of character.
7. Humbly asked him to remove our shortcomings.
8. Made a list of all persons we had harmed and became willing to make amends to them all.
9. Made direct amends to such people wherever possible, except when to do so would injure them or others.
10. Continued to take personal inventory and when we were wrong promptly admitted it.
11. Sought through prayer and meditation to improve our conscious contact with God *as we understood him,* praying only for knowledge of his will for us and for the power to carry that out.
12. Having had a spiritual awakening as a result of these Steps, we tried to carry this message to other alcoholics, and to practice these principles in all our affairs.

In the most basic sense, the challenges of recovering from a dysfunctional family background are quite different from those of recovering from alcoholism. However, there are important similarities—especially those dealing with issues of blame, responsibility and forgiveness—that make the use of the Twelve Steps effective in both realms.

Those addicted to alcohol and drugs typically start off blaming others for their troubles. They feel their problems are the fault of everyone but themselves. But these people also tend to be very self-condemning. They need to learn to take responsibility for their own lives, to forgive others—but also to forgive themselves.

Adult children from dysfunctional families, as we have seen, tend to start from the other end of the spectrum. They blame themselves for everything. As they come to grips with the realities of their past and discover ways in which they have been victimized, they can become quite bitter toward others. They need to learn to assign responsibility accurately for their problems, to forgive others and also to forgive themselves. Thus the recovery needs of the two groups end up being quite similar, at least in certain respects.

Let's take a look at the Twelve Steps and see how they relate to those of us who were raised in unhealthy dysfunctional homes.

STEP 1
We admitted we were powerless over our dependencies— that our lives had become unmanageable.

There is no question about it. As children of dysfunctional families, we were powerless indeed. This becomes evident as we work through the exercises in Part One of this book, where we looked at our families and how they operated. Those of us brought up in highly dysfunctional families have lived with craziness, both in our families and in ourselves. We have believed lies and myths, have helped maintain unhealthy secrets and have lived as if all of it were normal.

We are powerless. What happened to us is all in the past, out of reach. We have no power to change the past. Yet many of us spend a lifetime trying to do precisely that. We think that if we act a certain way, the past will be magically resolved. We must accept that we are powerless. Our injuries are there—there is nothing we can do to change that fact.

Many of us talk of wanting to make certain that the sins of the past do not recur in our present families. We work like crazy

to do things differently. Yet the harder we try, the more we seem to
repeat the past—if not in precisely the same way, at least in very
similar ways.

Recovery from wounds of the past always begins with accepting that we are *powerless* over the past. And then we realize we are
not helpless. We find that help in the next step.

STEP 2
Came to believe that a power greater than ourselves
could restore us to sanity.

There is a subtle but important truth here. The power we believe
in is "greater than ourselves," which means it must be *outside* ourselves. Many of us have become frustrated, trying to tap into a
power *within* ourselves. We do not realize that any power that
comes from within ourselves can be nothing more than an exten-
sion of ourselves, with all our evident weaknesses and limitations.
The only power that can restore us to sanity is one that is greater
than—and therefore outside of—ourselves.

When we ignore this reality and try to attain recovery in our
own strength, we end up frustrated, depressed, guilt-ridden and
ashamed. It is the very futility that fuels our craziness and removes
sanity ever further from our grasp.

STEP 3
Made a decision to turn our will and our lives over
to the care of God *as we understood Him.*

We begin to see how logical it is to turn our lives over to God. After all, we are dealing with issues of the past, and only God has the
ability to deal with them.

Turning our will and our lives over to God is foreign to us. As
adult children of dysfunctional families, our creed has always
been, "I can do it myself. I always have and I must continue to do
so!" It requires great courage and trust to let go. But we must give
to God our past with all its losses and shame, handing over every

moment of disgrace, every disappointment, every tear, every dashed hope, every scar.

We turn our lives over to God with the knowledge that He has offered us a relationship with Himself through His forgiveness of our failures. We find that God is able to make up for all we have lost. He can rid us of our shame and fill the empty places in our hearts.

From this we learn that resolution of problems rooted in the past can come only through forgiveness. When we make this third step, we begin down the pathway of forgiveness. First we *receive* God's forgiveness. In time, He will ask us to *extend* that forgiveness, both to others and to ourselves.

STEP 4
Made a searching and fearless moral inventory of ourselves.

Traditionally, this step has involved cataloging "the sins done *by* me," in recognition of the tendency of alcoholics and addicts to blame others for their problems. In breaking generational patterns, we also need to own up to our wrong actions.

At the same time, we must recognize that, by and large, we have been out of balance in the opposite direction. Having been emotionally, sexually or physically abused, or having been abandoned (or smothered) by family, we have spent years trying to figure out what *we* did to bring our pain upon ourselves.

For us, as for all those in recovery, it is important to make an inventory of the sins we have committed. But it is just as important to make an inventory of the sins done *to* us, the ways in which we have been victimized. We will need both inventories as we begin the process of forgiving others and ourselves.

STEP 5
Admitted to God, to ourselves, and to another
human being the exact nature of our wrongs.

Again, we must confess both the wrongs we have done *and* the wrongs that have been done to us.

First, we must confess to God. Then we must take a step that for many of us is far more difficult: We must admit to *ourselves* the truth of our inventories. For years, we have lived in denial. Many of us have idealized our families of origin. It is hard for us to face the truth, but it is essential to our recovery and our healing.

Second, we must take further action by confessing the truth to another person. So much of what wholeness is about (both in the Bible and in psychology) has to do with the principle of openness toward others. Not because they can do anything to change our situations, but because confession to another person makes real and concrete our rejection of the myths and lies that have held us bound. It reinforces our decision to leave behind the darkness of denial and to live in the light of truth.

We must be careful who we choose for this step. A therapist, a trusted friend, a minister or priest—any of these might be a good choice. A sibling who is walking alongside us in the same process of discovery and healing may also be appropriate.

STEP 6
Were entirely ready to have God remove all these defects of character.

It is our basic *willingness* that matters here, not the perfection of our inventories or the absolute purity of our intentions. Many of us worry whether we are "entirely" ready—our very desire to "do it right" stops us from doing it at all! Others of us (concerned that we must unearth every last detail of our past) set off on impossible "archaeological digs" through our childhood years, trying to specify *every* injury, every wound, no matter how minute.

This is a dead end. What matters is that we understand our brokenness and hunger for wholeness. When we know enough about our past to throw ourselves wholeheartedly into a quest for recovery through forgiveness, we know enough to take this step.

Again, a subtle adjustment in interpretation is in order. We must indeed be ready to sacrifice our own defects of character. But we must also be ready to forgive the defects of those who have harmed us.

Even in this, however, the focus is on ourselves. Our goal is not to *change* others, but to *accept* and *forgive* them. This is something that happens in *us*. Nothing in our working of the Twelve Steps will make any change in any other person. But the changes that can occur in us will make all the difference in the world.

STEP 7
Humbly asked God to remove our shortcomings.

Asking for anything can be a very difficult task for adult children of dysfunctional families. We may have grown up in situations where we were refused whatever we asked for or even punished for asking in the first place. This experience may have caused us to wall ourselves off from others, to seek a self-sufficiency that will prevent us from being hurt or disappointed again.

Now, however, we must learn to ask. We give up our willfulness and our need to control. We allow God to begin working the changes in our lives that we have been unable to produce in our own strength. We ask Him to remove not only our *shortcomings* but also what might be called our *short fallings*—the gaps in our development that are the result of our family's dysfunction.

STEP 8
Made a list of all persons we had harmed,
and became willing to make amends to them all.

Again, this step will cut in two directions for us. We must first work through the step as written: taking responsibility for the wrong things we have done, working through the process of repentance and taking responsibility for the consequences of our actions.

But we must also understand this step in another sense. We might restate it to read, "Made a list of all persons who had harmed us, and became willing to make peace with them all." In all cases, this willingness to make peace involves forgiving them, canceling the debt we hold against them. Whenever possible, it also involves seeking to be reconciled with them—bearing in mind that reconciliation is separate from forgiveness, and not under our control.

STEP 9
Made direct amends to such people wherever possible, except when to do so would injure them or others.

Here it is important to note that we must be careful not to add further injury to those who have hurt us. Our instincts may prompt us to confront those against whom we hold a grievance, without considering the consequences. But such behavior only makes our own pain worse.

We must come to see forgiveness as a process that takes time, so that we can patiently weigh each step and consider prayerfully how we ought to proceed. It is especially important at this point to have one or more "counselors" with whom we can discuss our plans.

We must also learn to discern our motives. Many times confrontation is motivated by a desire for vengeance, a desire to get even. We must always bear in mind that forgiveness, not revenge, is our aim.

STEP 10
Continued to take personal inventory and when we were wrong promptly admitted it.

How many times each day do we stop to check our appearance? To see that our face is clean, our hair in place, our clothes neat? How natural it is, then, that our recovery—our growth toward wholeness—involves a regular check-up on ourselves.

Our check-up has two facets. First, we check to see that we are taking appropriate responsibility for our own behavior. Second, we check to see that our boundaries are intact—that we are not allowing harmful people or patterns to creep back into our lives in ways we have come to see as dangerous.

Forgiveness is often a process that must be repeated. Even when we have worked through our feelings and forgiven someone who has hurt us, we may find that pain from old wounds starts showing up again, signaling us that fresh forgiveness may be in order.

STEP 11
Sought through prayer and meditation to improve
our conscious contact with God, as we understood Him,
praying only for knowledge of His will for us and
for the power to carry that out.

As we work through this process of forgiveness, we are able to move beyond ourselves and our pain, to establish a stronger, healthier relationship with God. Sometimes, as we are allowing ourselves to acknowledge and accept our pain, it feels as though God has forsaken us. The truth is that He is always walking alongside of us, helping us every step of the way.

One of the joys of forgiving is that we experience a wonderful freedom in our lives. Holding grudges keeps us focused on our pain—on ourselves. Forgiveness frees us to focus on God and on what His plan holds for us.

Recovery is a spiritual process. Our *forgiveness,* as we have seen, always flows from our *forgiven-ness*—from the mercy and grace that God has poured out upon us through His Son, Jesus. It builds on our relationship with God, as we come to know Him better and to walk more squarely in the heart of His plan for our lives.

STEP 12
Having had a spiritual awakening as a result
of these Steps, we tried to carry this message to others,
and to practice these principles in all our affairs.

Recovery can seem like a very self-focused exercise. But to be complete, it must focus on others as well. When we have been set free from the burden of a pain-filled past, it is only natural that we would want to share the freedom we have experienced with others. If we have included others in working these steps, it *will* be a natural part of the process to share our joy with others, especially with those who will benefit from walking the same path of forgiveness.

Having experienced forgiveness for our own wrongs and being able to extend forgiveness to others, we become new, free creatures. We move from codependency and dysfunctional behavior into genuine caring and love.

Note

1. The Twelve Steps are reprinted with permission of Alcoholics Anonymous World Service, Inc. Permission to reprint and adapt the Twelve Steps does not mean that Alcoholics Anonymous has reviewed or approved the contents of any publication that reprints the Twelve Steps, nor that Alcoholics Anonymous agrees with the views expressed therein. Alcoholics Anonymous is a program of recovery from alcoholism. Use of the Twelve Steps in connection with programs that are patterned after Alcoholics Anonymous but address other problems does not imply otherwise.

Small-Group and
Individual Study Guide

To gain the full benefit from the material contained in this book, it will be important for you to spend some time each day applying the things you have read to your own life and family situation.

If you will work through this study guide with an openness and sense of discovery, you will find yourself enlightened about the origin of your parents' dysfunction (considering their childhood influences), about the person you present to others and about the real you—the person who stares back at you from the mirror every day. You cannot change your past, but you can better understand its influences on you. This greater understanding will help you make choices to free you from the effects of the past, to make the most of your future and to develop healthier family relationships.

Chapter 1

Family: Ties that Bind?

Did you grow up in an unhealthy, dysfunctional family? For the purposes of this exercise, your "family" refers to the family in which you grew up. Answer the questions listed below truthfully and to the best of your recollection. Write your answers in a journal or notebook so that you can review them after you have completed the entire study guide.

1. Do the members of your family respect you and treat you like an adult when you are in their presence?
   a. If the answer is no, who is the person(s) that refuses to give you respect?
   b. Has he or she always dealt with you in this manner?
   c. Why do you think that person cannot accept you as a mature adult?

2. Is there one family member who seems to have control over everyone else?
   a. If so, does this person control by manipulation (convenient weakness or crisis that causes other family members to resume familiar roles) or by intimidation?
   b. How do you react internally to this person's controlling behavior?
   c. How do you react outwardly?
   d. If your outward behavior is different from your true feelings, what makes you react falsely? What are you afraid would happen if you expressed your true feelings?

3. Was it okay for you to express your feelings and opinions as a child?
   a. If not, what did you do with those feelings and opinions?
   b. Are you able to express your feelings and opinions now that you are an adult?

4. How did alcohol or drug abuse impact your childhood?
   a. Who in your immediate family abused alcohol or drugs?
   b. What specific crises arose for you because of the alcohol and drug abuse?
   c. How did you feel in the midst of these situations?

5. Were you or any of your family members mentally, physically or sexually abused?
   a. Was this abuse kept secret? If so, how did you deal with keeping such a secret?
   b. If you were abused, what have you done to seek help for yourself in resolving these issues and the emotional pain?
   c. If you were a witness to another's abuse, what have you done to deal with that?

6. What childhood memories do you carry that still bother you today?
   a. Do these memories, and any resulting inner turmoil, interfere with your ability to function normally in day-to-day life?
   b. Are you willing to look at those memories if necessary to get free of their negative influence?

7. What impact has growing up in a dysfunctional family had on your life?
   a. What is the negative impact?
   b. What positive impact has it had (as you have sought to overcome your past)?

Are you ready to break free from the bondage of your past? Are you ready to make a commitment to yourself, your healing and your future? If your answer to both of these questions is yes—even a hesitant yes—complete the information on the following personal contract and sign it as your personal commitment. It will

take commitment and tenacity to work through issues that may feel threatening or painful. You may want to share this contract with one supportive person who is not a member of your family system. You can then have someone to turn to for support as you make progress.

CONTRACTUAL AGREEMENT
FOR PERSONAL HEALING

I _____ do commit myself, this _____ day of _____ in the year _____, that I will give of myself whatever is necessary to achieve the healing I need and deserve. I make the following commitment to myself, depending on God's help, to do all that is within my power to face the truth about my family, work through the unresolved issues from my childhood and learn to forgive my parents and myself.

1. I will spend _____ minutes each day reflecting on the teaching in this book and considering how these teachings apply to my life.

2. I will post a journal entry each day, making a full effort to be open and honest about the feelings that begin to surface. I will record memories that seem pertinent to my healing process.

3. I will work to identify my own areas of dysfunction and to see where these may fit into the pattern of our family system. I will look to identify persons I have not yet forgiven, and try to understand how my family relationships may connect with my own dysfunctional habit patterns.

4. I am willing to stop blaming others for the way I live my life, even while acknowledging their influence. I will take full responsibility for my own healing process, with or without the support of my family.

5. I will begin to allow my true feelings to surface instead of pushing them down, and will note them in my journal as they come to mind.

6. If I find that I cannot work through these issues alone, I will seek the help of a support group or counselor.

Signed _____ Date _____

Witness (optional) _____ Date _____

CHAPTER 2

The Family System

You probably would not invest time reading this book if you didn't have family problems that you are looking to solve. You may have tried over and over again to resolve these problems without making much headway. One reason may be that you have been taking a cause-and-effect (linear) approach to a problem that is a "family system" problem, requiring an interactive approach. If so, there's good news: you don't have to try harder! You may just need to take a fresh look at your baffling family problems from a new perspective. Once you see the problem clearly from an interactive view, the solution may follow.

You can learn to take an interactive perspective by analyzing one of your baffling family problems. Once you learn how to look at one problem from this perspective and test these theories to see how they work, you can follow the same approach to deal with other problems.

As you work through these exercises, keep note of your feelings. If you are coming close to uncovering family secrets (even in your own mind) or debunking family myths, you will feel uncomfortable. Take note of these feelings by writing them in a journal or in your notes here. Those feelings are part of your research; they don't mean you should stop; rather, they may signal that you are getting close to the truth.

1. Think of one problem in your family that you would like to better understand and resolve. State briefly what the problem is and how you would like to see it resolved. (The example from the book would be: "Tracy keeps running away. I want to know why she is doing this, and get her to stop.")

   _____

   _____

   _____

   _____

   _____

2. Describe your theory about what is causing the problem by taking a linear perspective: Who is doing what and what is his or her problem (apart from family issues). Using our example from the book, you might say, "Tracy keeps running away. She is rebellious and probably using drugs or running with the wrong crowd." Now write about *your* problem from a linear perspective.

_____

_____

_____

_____

_____

3. How have you or other family members *reacted* to this problem behavior?

_____

_____

_____

_____

4. What positive results have you seen from your reactions that are based on a linear perspective?

_____

_____

_____

_____

5. What have you tried over and over to solve the problem that has not worked?

_____

_____

_____

_____

6. Consider the stories of Donna and Fred, or Joey and his parents in this chapter. Can you see any repeating patterns in your family that trouble you? If so, describe the *pattern* of interaction and who is involved in doing the same things over and over.

_____

_____

_____

_____

_____

_____

_____

7. Are you willing to put aside your previous theory about this problem and break the pattern of reactions to consider it in light of the family system? Are you willing to try to apply interactive thinking? If so, take the same problem you described above and try to describe it in the context of how that person connects with all the other players. Use the following questions to help you do so:

   a. What is going on in family relationships just prior to the problem occurring?

   · Is there a lifelong pattern of coping (like Fred's pattern of retreat under stress) that is repeated?

   · When the person (previously identified as having the problem) acts out, what typically happens? Does he or she get more attention, love, sympathy? Does it distract from something else that is going on?

   · What do various family members do in reaction to the "problem" behavior?

   · Is there a predictable payoff for the person who acts out? For instance, is stress relieved or pain averted or attention diverted from other problems in the family?

b. Considering all these angles, now describe the same problem in the context of family history and the family system.

_____

_____

_____

_____

8. In Joey's case, how might the payoff fill a legitimate need that is otherwise unmet in healthy ways? For instance: Joey may have been neglected while his mother hurried around the kitchen and his dad ignored him to watch TV.

_____

_____

_____

_____

9. Consider ways you might address any unmet needs directly or otherwise correct the family interaction to see what happens. What legitimate needs are not fully met that may play into this problem behavior?

_____

_____

_____

_____

10. Sometimes other family members can adapt to meet these needs in legitimate ways. This is not to placate or appease a person for problem behavior; rather it is to accept the problem as a family, consider what may contribute to the problem and work together to make the acting out unnecessary. How could other family members adapt to help meet unmet needs that may trigger the problem?

_____

_____

_____

_____

11. Linear thinking locks you into few choices in response to problems; interactive thinking opens up a world of possibilities for
positive change in your family system. Which has been your
primary way of looking at this problem? Are you willing to
practice rethinking every problem within your family as an interactive family problem?

_____

_____

_____

_____

_____

12. Picture your extended family seated around a large dinner
table. What is it that most everyone knows or certainly suspects
that no one would dare mention out loud?

_____

_____

_____

_____

13. What part may you be playing in maintaining the "conspiracy
of silence," and why?

_____

_____

_____

_____

_____

14. What would happen if you dared to state the family secrets out
in the open? (Who would faint, or have a heart attack, or be ru-
ined, or "just die!" or not be able to bear it?)

_____

_____

_____

_____

15. How has keeping the family secrets impacted your life? How do the fear and shame inhibit your life?

_____

_____

_____

_____

16. What family myths have been created to cover up or compensate for the family secrets?

_____

_____

_____

_____

17. How have they helped and hurt your family?

_____

_____

_____

_____

18. What family myths do you still support today?

_____

_____

_____

_____

19. What steps could you take to replace these myths with a healthy acceptance of the truth about your family?

_____

_____

_____

a. How could you accept the truth?

_____

_____

_____

b. How could you acknowledge the truth?

_____

_____

_____

_____

c. How could you express the truth?

_____

_____

_____

_____

20. Jesus Christ said, "You will know the truth, and the truth will set you free" (John 8:32). How could this apply to your family situation?

_____

_____

_____

_____

_____

CHAPTER 3

My Family and Me

1. The following are characteristics of a healthy family. Mark Y = yes, S = somewhat, or N = no to assess how healthy your family is now. For each one, cite an example to back up your assessment:

Adapts easily to change	Y	S	N
Well-defined boundaries	Y	S	N
Learn from one another	Y	S	N
Considerate of others' feelings	Y	S	N
Individuals take responsibility for own lives	Y	S	N
All problems seen as family problems	Y	S	N
Handle problems as a unit	Y	S	N
Deal directly with each other	Y	S	N
Encourage being individuals	Y	S	N
Tolerance for differences	Y	S	N
Expression of ups and downs okay	Y	S	N
Respect between generations	Y	S	N

2. I described four attachment styles in the chapter. One is the secure attachment, where the mother, and also the father to some extent, is available, responsive and accepting to the child. How would you rate your mother on these behaviors?

a. Mother was available in my preschool years, and this is how I experienced her availability:

_____

_____

_____

b. Mother was not available to me during those years, and this is how I experienced her not being available:

_____

_____

_____

c. Mother was responsive to me during my preschool years, and this is how I experienced her responsiveness:

_____

_____

_____

d. Mother was not responsive to me during these years, and this is how I experienced her as not being responsive:

_____

_____

_____

e. Mother was accepting of me during my preschool years, and this is how I experienced her acceptance:

_____

_____

_____

f. Mother was not accepting of me during these years, and this is how I experienced her not accepting me:

_____

_____

_____

_____

Do the same thing with your relationship with your father during your preschool years. Sometimes a father can make up for the deficits in our relationship with our mother. In what ways did you experience your father as available, responsive and/or accepting? In what ways was your experience of him as not being available, not being responsive and/or not being accepting?

_____

_____

_____

_____

_____

3. I identified three insecure attachment styles. They are the avoidant attachment style, the anxious/ambivalent attachment style and the fearful attachment style. If you do not believe that you had a secure attachment as a child, which of these three attachment styles would best describe you? Why?

_____

_____

_____

_____

_____

4. How has your predominant attachment style affected your adult relationships? Describe some of the issues you have faced based on your attachment style.

_____

_____

_____

_____

_____

5. Have you had any adult relationships that have helped you feel more secure in your attachments? Describe what you have experienced.

_____

_____

_____

6. If you had to classify your family as one of the following, which comes closest to describing your family?

   a. *Enmeshed*: Rigid Boundaries, keeping family members in by controlling each other's lives, and locking "non-members" out.

   b. *Disengaged*: Extreme lack of emotional support or bonding; very little togetherness in the family.

c. *Attached*: A healthy balance between enmeshed and disengaged. Members enjoy doing things together but also function well as individuals, apart from the family.

7. The following are descriptions of dysfunctional types. Does your family fit any of the following types?

a. *Isolated Islands:* All members are isolated from one another.

b. *Generational Splits:* Lack of significant interaction between generations.

c. *Gender Splits:* Lack of significant emotional interaction across the gender lines.

d. *Fused Pair:* Two members of the family cut themselves off from the rest of the family.

e. *Queen of the Hill:* This family is openly dominated by one person.

f. *Quiet Dictator:* One member completely controls the family with subtlety and manipulation. This person will usually refuse to participate in counseling.

g. *Family Scapegoat:* One family member accepts blame for anything that goes wrong in the family.

If you recognize dysfunctional family patterns, don't get discouraged. These realizations will help you make wise choices about how to become healthier, and encourage you to develop new patterns.

CHAPTER 4

The Sins of the Fathers

1. Create a genogram of your family, using the instructions found in this chapter. Go back at least two generations. You may not have all the information you need, but don't let that stop you. Start with what you do know and fill in as you gain more information.

2. After you have created your genogram, use it to answer the following questions:

   - What roles did you play in your family of origin?
   - Do you play the same roles now or have you taken on other familiar roles?
   - Who else played this role before you that you might be patterning yourself after—even unconsciously?
   - What unwritten rules are observed repeatedly in generation after generation?
   - What recurrent patterns do you see (consider those mentioned in the chapter: addiction, deception, codependency, adultery, divorce, desertion, abuse, playing favorites with children, lying)?

3. Create a family timeline (see page 83) describing the "horizontal axis" of your family life. Start with your marriage (or your birth if you are not married), and then chart all the various stressful events that have happened to members of your family.

4. Identify anything from your past that still bothers you, affects you, influences you or hinders you.

   _____

   _____

   _____

   _____

   _____

5. Using the definitions given and your genogram, identify the kind of boundaries you have in the following areas of your life. Circle the one that characterizes your typical behavior: R (rigid), D (diffuse), F (flexible). Remember: Rigid = too strong; Diffuse = too weak; flexible = healthy.

Individual personal boundaries   R   D   F
Intergenerational boundaries   R   D   F
Family boundaries   R   D   F

6. The following are unwritten rules that characterize dysfunctional families. Circle Y = yes, if this is characteristic of you; S = sometimes, if this is sometimes true of you; and N = no, if this is not true of you. If this is characteristic of other family member(s), write their names in the blank.

Y   S   N   Don't feel _____
Y   S   N   Always in control _____
Y   S   N   Deny what's going on _____
Y   S   N   Don't trust _____
Y   S   N   Keep family secrets _____
Y   S   N   Are ashamed _____

CHAPTER 5

Three-way Relationships

1. In which of your relationships do you and the other persons re-act to each other by habit instead of interacting spontaneously?

_____

_____

_____

2. Chart these relationships using the "triangle" method described in this chapter. Identify which type of triangle best represents each set of relationships:

   Ongoing continual patterns
   - All straight lines: Three people; solidly connected.
   - One straight and two wavy: Two people connect with one another against the third.

   Temporary, unstable patterns
   - All wavy lines: Three people who do not get along at all, or who cannot connect with each other.
   - Two straight and one wavy: One person, trying to hold together the other two who don't get along.

3. Look at these triangle models; then identify any hurt or anger re-sulting from these relational patterns. Below, list anyone from your triangles toward whom you harbor such feelings, and tell why.

_____

_____

_____

4. In each of the instances above, list specific ways your lack of for-giveness hinders *your* life today.

_____

_____

_____

5. How would you experience freedom if you could forgive each
   person on your list above?

   _____

   _____

   _____

6. Pages 100-101 refer to how a new person can uncover hidden
   dynamics when he or she enters into your family relationships.
   How has a third person (from outside your original family system) entered a relationship with you and been able to blow the
   cover off your denial systems?

   _____

   _____

   _____

   _____

   What fresh perspective on your family did this person bring to
   your attention?

   _____

   _____

   _____

   _____

   What reaction occurred within the family system that tried to
   return the relationships to the way they were before?

   _____

   _____

   _____

   Did you give in to the pressure of the family system to restore
   the denial, or form new relationships within the system? Why
   or why not?

   _____

   _____

   _____

   _____

CHAPTER 6

Forgiving Others, Releasing Ourselves

1. This chapter asserts that "forgiveness is the only way to attain genuine freedom from the bad effects of the past." Before you can begin to forgive, you must recognize and acknowledge how you have been hurt by wrongs done to you. It is common in dysfunctional families to pretend not to be hurt. How have you felt pressured not to acknowledge the hurts that have injured you in your family?

   _____

   _____

   _____

   _____

2. Refer to your genogram and triangle models of your relationships. Use these to help you compile a list of wrongs done to you. This is a process that will take time. Use the spaces below to list any that come to mind immediately. Use a journal to list other memories as they surface. Wrongs done to me:

   1. _____
   2. _____
   3. _____

   (Start with the three most pressing incidents. Once you learn the process to forgive these, you can repeat the process for all the rest of the wrongs that remain to be forgiven.)

3. For each of the wrongs done to you (above) identify those people who hurt you and those who didn't protect you from hurt:

Those who hurt me	Those who didn't protect me
#1: _____	_____
#2: _____	_____
#3: _____	_____

4. Unforgiveness is characterized by feeling "as though they have taken away something that belonged to us—our peace, our joy, our happiness—and that they now owe it to us." This chapter used the analogy of holding an emotional IOU toward those who hurt you. Take a separate piece of paper for each of the persons you named above. Make out an IOU that represents what you are holding against them, what they did, how that robbed you of something and what you feel they owe you (if they had the power to give it back). Hold on to these until you finish with them further on.

———————————————————————————————
———————————————————————————————
———————————————————————————————
———————————————————————————————

5. Many people refuse to forgive because they think forgiveness means they must forget what happened, act as if it was okay or act as though it didn't hurt them. Does understanding that forgiveness includes acknowledging wrong and canceling the debt help you become willing to forgive? Why or why not?

———————————————————————————————
———————————————————————————————
———————————————————————————————
———————————————————————————————
———————————————————————————————

6. Forgiveness starts with a personal decision. If you are willing to begin the process of forgiveness toward those named on your emotional IOUs, sign your commitment below: I choose to forgive. I commit myself to begin this process of forgiveness today:

Signature: _____

Date: _____

Remember, you will need to express the feelings associated with the injuries you have suffered. You may not *feel* like you are in the process of forgiveness. Whenever you doubt your commitment, look at your signature here and reaffirm your commitment to work through all the steps of forgiveness.

7. Look at each of the IOUs you have created to represent those you need to forgive. For each of these, identify the emotions stirred up when you dare to think about what happened and how it hurt you. In your journal, complete the following sentences to help you identify your emotions for each IOU you made:

    a.   I am afraid to look at this because . . .
    b.   I feel guilty about . . .
    c.   I feel ashamed and humiliated by . . .
    d.   I am angry that . . .
    e.   I feel sad because . . .

8. "Expressing your destructive emotions is important because it gets them 'out of your system' so that they cannot poison you any longer." Choose how you will express your emotions related to each of the emotional IOUs you have created. I will:

    ____   Talk them out
    ____   Write them out
    ____   Talk to an empty chair
    ____   Other: _____

Take time now to work on expressing your emotions associated with one of your IOUs. You can work through the others as you are able.

9. How have your boundaries been violated as you were growing up in your family?

_____

_____

_____

_____

_____

10. What new boundaries do you need to set to protect yourself?

_____

_____

_____

_____

11. This is the time in the process to cancel the debt or transfer it to God. It may help you cancel the debt to know that you can transfer that person's account to God for Him to settle as He sees fit. Even if the person has not repented or acknowledged how he or she has hurt you, you can let go of your demands that the person make up to you what you feel he/she owes you. After you have worked through steps 1-4, as explained in this chapter, for any of the IOUs that represent what you were holding against someone, choose to cancel that debt or turn it over to God. Write "CANCELED" across the IOU and date it to symbolize your release of that person's offenses against you.

12. Consider the possibilities of reconciliation. Answer the following questions for each person with whom you are considering reconciliation. Use your answers to help you decide where the relationship goes from here. Remember, to forgive someone does not mean you *have* to reconcile the relationship.

   • Why do you want reconciliation?
   • If you approach the other person, what do you think his/her response will be?
   • Can you accept the worst possible response?
   • How can you check to see if the other person is open to working through his/her part of the reconciliation?

13. What is your next step to prepare yourself and move toward reconciliation?

_____

_____

_____

_____

CHAPTER 7

Forgiving and Forgetting

1. List two things you gain from remembering and accepting a past hurt, even though you've forgiven it.

1. _____

2. _____

2. Use these sentence starters to help you cite a specific example from your life.

When I remembered . . .

_____

_____

_____

_____

_____

It helped me . . .

_____

_____

_____

_____

3. Your current problems may relate to past hurts that have not been fully resolved. List a few of your current problems below, and then see if you can trace the problem back to a previous hurt.

Current problem	**Past hurt**
Example: I am insecure and suspicious.	My spouse had an affair.
1. _____	_____
2. _____	_____
3. _____	_____

4. What past experiences have you had to try not to think about because they trouble you?

_____

_____

_____

_____

5. What kind of emotions do you experience when you allow these repressed thoughts to surface?

_____

_____

_____

_____

6. Are you willing to notice when you are trying *not* to think about something, face the feelings and deal with what happened so you can work through them? _____

7. Is there any period of time during your childhood that is missing from your memory? If so, consider each of the time periods listed below. For each age range in your life, try to recall what life was like during these years—where you were living, what your room looked like, what was going on at home and at school. Circle any of these age ranges where you cannot remember details.

Ages: 1–4   5–8   9–12   13–15   16–18

These blank spots in your memory may give you clues to painful parts of your past that you have not resolved.

8. Consider how you describe your father and mother to others. Do you tend to paint them as all good or all bad?

_____

_____

_____

_____

9. Try to write down a description about your parents that includes at least three good characteristics and three bad characteristics.

_____

_____

_____

_____

_____

If you have trouble doing this, you may want to explore this further with the help of a counselor.

10. Which best describes your view of your parents?

- Outright rejection
- Unhealthy idealization
- Healthy realization that they are only human—good and bad

11. Can you identify your mother in one of the following types?

- *Intrusive*: Very controlling; uses guilt trips; lacks respect for healthy boundaries in your life
- *Abandoning*: Either physically or emotionally absent
- *Unpredictable*: Sometimes loving, sometimes cold and indifferent

12. Looking back over your childhood, can you now see where you may have thought that you were bad, because you could not conceive that your parents could be the ones at fault? How have you condemned yourself unjustly?

_____

_____

_____

_____

_____

13. What crutches have you leaned on to cope with and escape the pain of your life?

_____

_____

_____

_____

_____

_____

14. How have you used *controlling* behavior, living in *denial, avoidance* of uncomfortable situations or memories, and existing in a state of emotional *numbness* to escape your inner pain?

_____

_____

_____

_____

_____

15. When have you been in hurtful situations but were forbidden to acknowledge what was happening and express your anger? How does this still influence your ability to express anger when anger is justified?

_____

_____

_____

_____

_____

16. What have you learned from the pain of the past that can help protect you from being "burned" again?

_____

_____

_____

17. This chapter said, "We forgive—even as we remember!" Are you willing to do so? If so, how are you actively doing this?

_____

_____

_____

_____

_____

_____

18. Are you willing to seek the help of a professional therapist, if necessary, to aid you in the process of remembering what happened, facing the feelings that arise and completing the process of forgiveness? _____

CHAPTER 8

What's Anger Got to Do with It?

1. Is it difficult for you to recognize, admit or deal with your anger? Why or why not?

_____

_____

_____

_____

_____

_____

2. How does this show itself in your family relationships?

_____

_____

_____

_____

_____

3. Do you accept what this chapter asserts: that it is not only okay, but necessary to recognize and accept your anger before you will be able to truly forgive? _____

4. If accepting anger as being okay to feel is new for you, how can you remind yourself of this when you automatically try to ignore or stuff your angry feelings?

_____

_____

_____

_____

_____

5. Resentment is the by-product of unexpressed anger. Toward whom do you hold resentment? (If you're not sure, it's those

people who stir up anger or other repressed emotions when you see them or think about them.)

_____

_____

_____

_____

_____

6. Unexpressed anger and the resentment it causes become a poison if they are not acknowledged and dealt with on a conscious level. Are you willing to do the work of expressing the anger and resentment you currently have buried? If so, which of the methods listed below will you use:

   • Write down exactly how you feel
   • Share your feelings with a trusted friend
   • Verbalize your feelings out loud to yourself
   • Write a letter to the person (but *don't* send it)

7. When do you hide your angry feelings because you feel guilty? For example, you "have no right to feel angry." Who convinced you that you have no right to feel angry?

_____

_____

_____

_____

8. When do you hide your angry feelings because you are afraid to express them? What are you afraid will happen if you express your anger?

_____

_____

_____

_____

9. Some people from dysfunctional families learn to negate their feelings. The "good" feelings are allowed to be acknowledged and expressed, but the emotions that are considered "bad" have to be squashed. Rate each of the following emotions on a scale of 1-10 (1 = not accepted at all, 10 = fully acceptable).

fear	1	2	3	4	5	6	7	8	9	10
frustration	1	2	3	4	5	6	7	8	9	10
hurt	1	2	3	4	5	6	7	8	9	10
sadness	1	2	3	4	5	6	7	8	9	10
anger	1	2	3	4	5	6	7	8	9	10
happiness	1	2	3	4	5	6	7	8	9	10

10. While all emotions are part of being human, there are acceptable and unacceptable ways of expressing them. What are some acceptable ways in which you can express the feelings you previously considered unacceptable?

_____

_____

_____

_____

_____

11. Will you make a commitment *not* to consciously repress your feelings of anger, but rather face and express them in a constructive way?

_____

_____

_____

_____

12. It takes practice to learn to recognize your anger and express it in appropriate ways. One good guideline is to talk out your feelings with someone you trust, but wait before expressing your anger to the person to whom the anger is directed. Is there

someone you trust with whom you could discuss your angry
feelings prior to taking any further action? Who?

_____

_____

_____

_____

13. There are four common ways people tend to deal with anger.
Which best describes you?

_____ 1. You repress your anger until you explode.
_____ 2. You immediately vent your anger to the person
with whom you are angry.
_____ 3. You realize and acknowledge your anger but opt
to count to 10 before reacting.
_____ 4. You discuss your anger with someone that you
trust in an attempt to understand why you feel as
you do and how best to handle the anger.

Only numbers 3 and 4 are healthy ways of dealing with your
anger. What can you do to begin reacting in a healthier way
with regard to a specific incident about which you are angry?

_____

_____

_____

_____

_____

14. "Forgiveness is a journey of many steps." What steps have you
taken so far?

_____

_____

_____

_____

What steps can you take next to find or work through your anger in healthy ways to move you along on the path of forgiveness?

_____

_____

_____

_____

_____

CHAPTER 9

The Blame Game

1. When something bad happens in your life, do you have the tendency to blame someone else? _____

2. Blaming others is often a cover-up for fear. What are you afraid of that prompts you to look for someone to blame: punishment, embarrassment, responsibility or what?

   _____

   _____

   _____

   _____

   _____

   _____

3. Do you accept that "stuff just happens" sometimes or do you always have to look for someone to blame when something goes wrong?

   _____

   _____

   _____

   _____

   _____

4. With whom do you need to break out of a circular dance of blaming?

   _____

   _____

   _____

   _____

5. God limited vengeance in the Old Testament to "an eye for an eye, and a tooth for a tooth." Are there limits to your desire for

vengeance or does it seem insatiable? If so, what limits do you put on your desire for vengeance?

_____

_____

_____

_____

6. What are some things you can do to put the bad or disappointing times in your life into the proper perspective?

_____

_____

_____

_____

7. What is the difference between (a) blaming and (b) remembering a past offense while acknowledging the truth of what happened?

_____

_____

_____

_____

_____

8. Judging from past experience, has placing blame on someone else ever helped you move past the issue and away from bitterness? _____

9. Explain why it is good for you to begin the process of forgiveness, even when the offender may not deserve your forgiveness; include the benefits if you stop blaming someone else for your present condition:

_____

_____

_____

_____

_____

10. If you find yourself stuck in a pattern of blaming others, are you willing to seek professional counsel to help you stop blaming and start accepting responsibility for your own life?

_____

_____

_____

_____

_____

11. Look at the model on page 180. Which path are you on, and where are you along that path?

_____

_____

_____

_____

_____

12. What tendencies of a "codependent" person described in this chapter do you exhibit?

_____

_____

_____

_____

13. Is there anyone in your life who makes it easier for you to continue unhealthy patterns of living by his or her codependent behavior? If so, what are you willing to do to bring your relationship with your enabling partner into a healthier pattern of relating?

_____

_____

_____

_____

_____

14. Are you willing to practice speaking your feelings in "I" state-
    ments, rather than "You" statements? If so, to whom will you
    make this commitment so he/she can help you monitor the
    way you speak and how you tend to place blame on others?

    _____

    _____

    _____

    _____

    _____

    _____

15. List the names of the people with whom you currently share
    your feelings and troubles.

    _____

    _____

    _____

    _____

    _____

    _____

    Do these people tend to join your pity party or help you move
    along the path of forgiveness and accepting responsibility for
    your life?

    _____

    _____

    _____

    _____

16. How does each of the persons listed above either help you move
    out of blaming or join you in blaming?

    _____

    _____

    _____

    _____

17. How can you change the nature of your relationships away from blaming and choose people who will not encourage you to blame others?

_____

_____

_____

_____

_____

_____

CHAPTER 10

Confrontation and/or Reconciliation

1. Forgiveness and reconciliation are separate but closely related issues. Make a list here of all the people with whom you are somewhere in the process of forgiveness or reconciliation:

   _____

   _____

   _____

   _____

   _____

   _____

   • Now draw a circle around any names on the list of those whom you have forgiven but with whom you have not been reconciled.
   • Next, draw a box around any names of those with whom you have reconciled without true forgiveness.
   • Put a star next to the names of those with whom you have reconciled and forgiven.
   • Draw a check next to the names of those you have forgiven and done all you can to reconcile (even if they have refused to reconcile).

2. Have you been holding yourself responsible for a lack of reconciliation in cases where you have done all you can? _____ If so, will you stop taking responsibility for the other person's decision? _____

3. Look at the names you drew a box around—those with whom you reconciled without going through the process of forgiveness. In each instance, did you:

   _____ Overlook the pain caused by someone else's actions?
   _____ Deny that you were hurt?
   _____ Excuse the inexcusable behavior?

_____ Fear that you would lose the relationship if you spoke up?

_____ Fear _____ if you spoke up?

4. In situations where you are seeking reconciliation, are you ready to bring forward the hidden things that need to be brought to light? _____

5. What are your motives in wanting to confront or deal with these issues?

_____ Retaliation	_____ To bring the truth to light
_____ Revenge	_____ To seek reconciliation
_____ Retribution	_____ To restore relationship
_____ Spitefulness	_____ To help me forgive completely

(Note: If you answered yes to any of the reasons on the left, wait on any confrontation. When your motives move into the column on the right, you are ready for a confrontation that can lead to reconciliation.)

6. Confrontation calls for careful preparation. What will you do to prepare yourself to confront those you believe you need to confront?

_____

_____

_____

_____

7. Can you go into a confrontation with no expectations about the outcome of the meeting? _____ What expectations do you have? What do you hope for but don't necessarily expect?

_____

_____

_____

_____

8. Are you prepared to handle the following reactions:

_____ Denial (*That isn't what happened.*)
_____ Counter-charging (*It's your fault.*)
_____ Minimizing the issue (*It wasn't that bad.*)
_____ Ambiguity (*I don't remember it like that.*)

Practice how you would handle each of these reactions if you were to confront the issue.

9. Do you need to work through forgiveness and reconciliation with someone who is dead? If so, what technique will you use to help you do so?

_____

_____

_____

_____

_____

_____

10. Are you in a situation where the person who hurt you as a child has changed and is no longer the type of person who would still hurt you? If so, can you acknowledge and forgive what he/she did in the past while dealing with the person as he/she is now?

_____

_____

_____

_____

_____

CHAPTER 11

Forgiving My Parents, Forgiving Myself

1. Are you willing to consider how your attitudes and choices (about how to deal with what happened to you) contributed to your pain? _____

2. List the ways (if any) in which you have added to your own pain.

   _____

   _____

   _____

   _____

   _____

3. Are you ready and willing to forgive yourself for the things you have listed above? _____

4. You will need to work through the steps listed below to be ready to forgive yourself:

   a. Recognize the injury . . .

   What happened?

   _____

   _____

   _____

   _____

   _____

   What role did you play?

   _____

   _____

   _____

   _____

   _____

Did you do anything wrong?

_____

_____

_____

b. Identify the emotions involved. Do you feel . . .

_____ fear
_____ guilt
_____ shame
_____ anger
_____ sadness
_____ other

5. Which of the following techniques will you use to express your feelings about how you have contributed to your own pain?

_____ talk them over with a friend
_____ write out what happened
_____ talk to myself about it

6. Are any of the following conditions a sign that you lack boundaries?

_____ compulsive overeating
_____ starving myself
_____ abuse of alcohol or drugs
_____ overdoing exercise
_____ engaging in dangerous behavior
_____ become antagonistic
_____ other: _____

A yes answer to any of these conditions will lead to further injury and self-loathing if left unchecked. What will you do to deal with any of these problem areas?

_____

_____

_____

_____

7. Are you ready to cancel the debt that you hold against yourself? _____

8. Which of the following statements of self-forgiveness can you agree with?

_____ I am no longer willing to blame myself.
_____ I am no longer willing to accept guilt over what happened.
_____ I did the best I could with the knowledge I had.
_____ I will be compassionate toward myself.
_____ I am human. I will make mistakes.

9. Are you willing to pray and ask God to forgive you all your sins and shortcomings, and to accept the payment Jesus Christ made on the cross to pay for all your sins? _____ If so, giving consideration to everything listed above, can you and do you choose to forgive yourself? _____

10. Make a replica of the emotional IOU you have held against yourself. Write "CANCELED" across it when you have chosen to forgive yourself, and date it. You have shown your determination to forgive and find healthier patterns of relating by conscientiously working through this study guide. Remember, it's okay to seek help. When you are dealing with patterns of life that have molded your thinking from childhood, you may need the help of a counselor to work through these issues. Don't be afraid or embarrassed to ask for help. If you find yourself stuck on any of the exercises given here, please seek help from a qualified professional you can trust.